Portrait of
THE RIVER MEDWAY

by

Roger Penn

ILLUSTRATED
AND WITH MAP

ROBERT HALE · LONDON

© *Roger Penn 1981*
First published in Great Britain 1981

ISBN 0 7091 9434 X

Robert Hale Limited
Clerkenwell House
Clerkenwell Green
London EC1R 0HT

Photoset by Rowland Phototypesetting Limited
Printed in Great Britain by
St Edmundsbury Press, Bury St Edmunds, Suffolk
Bound by Weatherby Woolnough Ltd

Contents

Illustrations

PICTURE CREDITS

The author and publishers thank the following for permission to reproduce illustrations: Institute of Geological Sciences, London (no. 2); Mr M. V. C. Williams, the Headmaster (no. 3); Courier Newspapers, Tunbridge Wells (no. 10); Alfred Reader & Co., Teston (no. 22); Reed Paper & Board U.K. Ltd (no. 25); B.P. Oil, Kent Refinery, Ltd (no. 32); Medway Ports Authority (no. 37). All other photographs were taken by the author.

MAP

To Danae and Carolyn

1

Introduction to a River

Rivers are not unlike humans: some are great individuals, while many others share their characteristics like the long slow rivers that flow over vast continents. Smaller lands with many a hill and vale may have more individual rivers that reflect the sudden change of scene, as with the many short rivers of southern England that flow through pleasant rural and interesting urban surroundings.

But for sheer variety of landscape it would be difficult to find a better river valley than the Medway in its seventy miles from high Sussex through the changing scenery of Kent to the Thames estuary. The main reason for this variety is that the river's course for the greater part of its life lies across the Weald, a landscape of a series of concentric belts of country overlooked by the Chalk Downs. The source region is amid the beautiful hilly wooded sandy ridges and clay vales of the Sussex High Weald; then comes a wide flat plain of clay, followed by the river cutting through a narrower ridge of sandy limestone and finally sawing a great gap through the chalk to reach the marshes of a wide tidal estuary.

The evolution of this landscape is far back in geological time, and what we see now is only the climax of a process spanning many millions of years. The sands and clays of the High Weald were once the sandy deltas and muddy bottom of a great freshwater lake, along the shores of which, amid a primitive forest of conifers like the present-day monkey-puzzle or Chile pine and ancient palms called cycads, ferns and horse-tail swamps, were iguanodons. These huge, rather harmless, lizard-like dinosaurs were herbivores that browsed on the lakeside plants. In 1933 some pelvic bones of one were found at the High Brooms brickworks, near Tunbridge Wells. In the lake, wallowing at a safe distance from its predators, would be the enormous 80-foot (24-metre) amphibian known as diplodocus—the water supporting its huge bulk. Far more terrifying flying overhead were the primitive ancestors of modern birds called pterodactyls; these were flying reptiles with scaly wings, fearsome teeth and claws, rather like the flying dragons of Chinese paintings.

The Wealden district eventually became a great dome-shaped

upfolding of the earth's crust that has had its top worn away. When this dome was first uplifted, rivers—of which the Medway's ancestor was one—flowed outwards from the middle, cutting channels like the spokes of a wheel. These were the precursor valleys of the present ones cut in the chalk of the North and South Downs.

Now was revealed the older sandstones and clays of the High Weald, and the chalk slowly retreated to make the familiar crests or scarps along the edges of the Downs.

Nearer to our own times the Weald was invaded by a shallow sea which left the middle of it as an island with the rivers and streams still carving away the rocks as they flowed northwards to this new sea.

When at length the sea level fell these rivers, including the ancestor of the Medway, pushed their courses out across the new sea floor, and so the line of the present northern Weald rivers was established with vales being cut into the soft clays. The Medway cut a gap in the Greensand Ridge between Yalding and Maidstone and in order to maintain its course sawed its way through the North Downs between Aylesford and Rochester.

One more great event was to affect the landscape and its rivers; this was the Ice Age with huge ice sheets that waxed and waned for over a million years. The Weald itself was not actually glaciated, for the ice front stopped north of the Downs, but small snow- and ice-fields glinted in the weak sunshine on the chalk crests and sandstone hills.

During this period there were many rises and falls of sea level as the climate varied from icy conditions to warm wetter periods when heavy rain swelled the rivers which were wearing away the landscape far more heavily than today. The Wealden rivers responded to the changes and their courses wandered, cutting down deeply, and later swilling huge amounts of gravel, sands and pebbles from their swollen channels. Today, as a result, the Medway and its tributaries like the Eden, Teise and Beult are bordered by a whole series of gravel terraces. Another effect was that the more powerful rivers and their tributaries full of melt-water cut their headwaters back and thus captured those of the weaker streams. The Medway tributaries captured the Darenth westwards and the Great Stour eastwards, whilst the Lower Teise did the same to the Upper Teise near Goudhurst.

A few thousand years ago the ice retreated at last from British shores and we reach the present day with the Medway flowing as a tiny stream outwards from the edge of Ashdown Forest in

Sussex, then eastwards through Forest Row in a typical Wealden vale to near Groombridge, gathering much water from the many small rushing streams coming down the slopes of Ashdown Forest. Into Kent and turning north, the Medway winds through to Penshurst in deeply cut bends, where it is joined by the Eden—equally sinuous and with steep banks. Onwards it flows as a sizeable river now to Tonbridge where the High and Low Weald meet; again it turns eastwards and flows across the claylands of the flat Low Weald, collecting the waters of the Shode, Teise and Beult on the way, to Yalding before cutting its gap through the Greensand Ridge to Maidstone.

At the county town its waters are increased by the tiny fast-flowing Loose and the larger but slower Len from Mote Park. Then it turns north for the last time and carves a great breach through the chalk to Rochester, and curving round in great reaches it enters its broad tidal estuary with a flourish, and finally loses itself in the Thames at Sheerness and is borne with the mother river into the North Sea.

But the story of a river is also that of man along its banks, and the most ancient marks of Medway man are probably in the famous Old Stone Age rock shelters at Oldbury, near Ightham. However, early man was a rare creature and near the end of the Old Stone Age he lived closer to the river bank, for among the remains of the mammoth, woolly rhinoceros and reindeer in the Medway's oldest terrace at Aylesford are flint implements.

By now the ice was retreating, but it was still cold along that Medway of 10,000 years ago, and these primitive people of a primitive Kent still joined to Artois in an equally primitive France must have been tough to survive the climate and to live at all. Their lives would have been as Thomas Hobbes wrote in his *Leviathan* of the seventeenth century: "No arts; no letters; no society; and the life of man, solitary, poor, nasty, brutish and short . . ."

Time passed, the climate warmed up and about 5,000 years ago reached its peak, not repeated since, as our recent dismal summers remind us. The Straits of Dover were breached for the last time, and the Medway valley was richly wooded with oaks and alder. The great Wealden forest of southern England was thick, impenetrable and little disturbed, and would remain so until well into Saxon times. The Medway dwellers lived near the edge of the forest and beside a river rich in fish. They still hunted, although with dogs now; but their wandering lives have left little trace except for their stone tools.

Then came a great change, for from Holland and North Germany small groups of people braved the sea and crossed into England using the Medway and other rivers. This was the great New Stone Age, or Neolithic Folk movement, which brought farming, stockbreeding, crude pottery and burial in barrows and chambered stone tombs, with later the use of metals—gold and copper. The valley of the Medway along the Chalk Downs between Maidstone and Rochester is particularly rich in their monuments, and the primitive use of metal from the rich copper and sporadic iron deposits led into the Bronze and Iron Ages which changed life along the river from isolated settlements into populated villages and forts.

Then in 100 B.C. the first of the invasions of the Belgae took place. They were Celtic warriors from Gaul (present-day Belgium) and reached Kent by what was now a regular water route—the Medway. They settled in the valley below Maidstone and later some moved north across the Thames. The second group were rather more determined people who built defended settlements and clashed with the native British Celts in their hill forts. But all this brought an Iron Age Industrial Revolution, for the Belgae had the wheel, industrialized pottery-making and eased the housewife's chore of grinding corn by using a rotary quern which made fine flour. They even had a system of high finance with gold, silver and bronze coins stamped with their leaders' names—the first real British names that have come down to us. The rich soils of the Medway valley were used to grow corn—enough even for export. Evidence of the high level of Belgae culture came to light once again at Aylesford. This was the discovery of the famous decorated bronze and wood "Aylesford bucket" (now in the British Museum).

But a new era was fast approaching when in 55 B.C. a clean-shaven soldier in armour holding aloft a bronze eagle waded through the surf at Walmer—the Romans had arrived! At first, however, it was merely a test of strength between Julius Caesar and the chief tribe of the Catuvellani, and an uneasy peace was maintained for some years. These Celts were already partly Romanized through trade, so changes were inevitable; some Celts may even have welcomed them. The final conquest came in A.D. 43, the climax of which was a two-day battle near the Belgic settlement of Durobrivae—now Rochester. The Roman army surprised the defenders by using tough Batavian soldiers from Holland to swim the Medway and secure a bridgehead for the 2nd August Legion, who attacked, gained the day, and forged on to subdue the Catuvellani at Colchester.

Within a short time the Roman penetration of the Medway brought one of the most flourishing Romano-British settlements, with many villas—some in the same area as the old Neolithic monuments like Kit's Coty. A regular waterborne trade on the river developed, and the Medway became a very civilized river, with these people of the Roman Kent probably much nearer to ourselves than the people of later Saxon or Jutish Kent in the period that followed Rome.

After four centuries of law and a fair amount of order along the river Rome withdrew and the Medway was left to the Germanic raiders lurking in the North Sea. The next five centuries produced waves of many varied Teutonic people from the Rhine to Norway, at first by hit-and-run raids, then full-scale armies invading, and later more peaceful settlements. But out of all this came a Christianized kingdom of Kent, apart from the rest of England, which developed a great flowering of Frankish culture of which the Medway valley was no small part.

In the eleventh century came another great change with the Norman Conquest, and the Medway became an ordered river defended by great castles at Tonbridge and Rochester with the river once again being used for commerce from Maidstone to the Yantlet, as Kentish ragstone went to build the Tower of London.

The medieval period saw the decline of upstream navigation and much of the river was given over to mills and fishing, eels in particular. Magna Carta in 1215 was aware of the problem and states: "All kiddles (weirs fitted with nets to catch fish) and weirs from henceforth shall be utterly put down by Thames and Medway." But these obstructions remained, and in the long period between the Middle Ages and the 1740s the river was more important for water power than water transport. Between 1600 and 1665 the river between Yalding and Tonbridge was said to be "littered with weirs and tree trunks", but the great importance of the Wealden iron industry in Kent and Sussex meant that the Medway was sometimes used to transport the cannon to the Royal dockyards, after a long and painful slog through the Wealden mud.

Downstream, however, the river was always alive with a great variety of shipping and working river craft—small sailing vessels like hoys from Maidstone, barges of all kinds and, later, Whitby colliers coming to Rochester. The dockyards developed from the nearness of London and the depth of water in the good anchorages off Chatham and Sheerness, so warships began to become part of the Medway scene and the long association that the river has had with the Royal Navy and Royal Marines.

But war came to the river too, with the Kentish Royalist uprising in 1648 and the disastrous Dutch raids twenty years later when the sad disgrace of the burning and capture of the King's ships was seen by the citizens of the Medway towns.

Early in the nineteenth century the Medway might have seen another invasion, this time by Napoleon, as his plan was to land at Deal and march along Watling Street to Rochester, but it needed a genius of the sea like Nelson to control the Straits, rather than the pessimistic, over-cautious Villeneuve. Nevertheless there have always been garrisons at Maidstone and Chatham, and the Army is still part of the Medway story today, represented by the Royal Engineers and their School at Chatham of Royal Military Engineering.

Then came the railway era and many bridges were built across the river from Tonbridge through Yalding to Maidstone and finally at Rochester, which for a long time had two bridges —reflecting the great rivalry between the two Kentish companies. The valley between Yalding and Strood was used for a line that still makes one of the best ways to see the river even today.

In both world wars the Medway saw action; in the first war with Naval airships based on the Hoo peninsula and large units of the Fleet anchored in the estuary, and the occasional air raid by Zeppelins and later the far more dangerous and lethal attacks by the huge biplane Gothas, based near Ostende. In the second war the river came into the front line with German bombers using the line of the river to attack London, and great aerial dogfights raged above the middle and upper valley.

Since the war has come the reorganization of the water authorities; tributary valleys have been flooded to provide reservoirs, and a great flood-control scheme has been built near Tonbridge after the local disasters of September 1968. The great tidal surge of 1953 left its mark on the estuary lands, particularly the Isle of Sheppey, and much-needed flood defences have been built and improved.

The estuary has seen the greatest changes with oil and the consumer society, for now the largest type of vessel, the supertanker, is seen in the river and curious-looking vessels like car ferries, car transporters and container ships throng the wharves and deep-water berths of the up and coming new commercial port of Sheerness.

Sadder perhaps for older people has been the slow and painful demise of the Navy, and grey-hulled warships are now rather a rarity instead of the common sight they once were; but the sinister shapes of nuclear submarines slip out of Chatham along with the occasional frigate to show that the Navy is still alive and kicking—but different.

For the best era of building along the river we must return to the late eighteenth and early and mid-nineteenth century, when the Medway valley was the scene of the genius of five famous architects and landscapers: Benjamin Latrobe, Humphrey Repton, Decimus Burton, George Devey, and Norman Shaw, who built and embellished in or near villages like Forest Row, Groombridge, Penshurst and towns like Tonbridge and Tunbridge Wells.

And for over two thousand years the banks of the river and its tributaries have been cultivated for corn, vines, orchards and hops; fruit grows from Penshurst and the Eden valley right down to the wide estuary at Lower Halstow and the Hoo peninsula, and vineyards are once again adorning the valley—a far-off heritage from Rome.

Part I

SUSSEX—THE UPPER RIVER

2

The Source and Headwaters

Rivers are probably the oldest features of the natural landscape that have names; certainly in Europe nearly all river names are of great antiquity, and are usually of Celtic origin. In France three of her main rivers—the Seine, Marne and Saône—all bear names derived from river goddesses inspired by a Celtic cult of Druidesses, and in Britain the river Severn is named from a water goddess called Sabrina. But those who named the Medway apparently had other ideas, for it is a compound name, whose first element comes from the Celtic *Medu* meaning mead, and the second refers to the water itself. The whole name means perhaps: "river with sweet water"—which is a nice thought, for early man's water supply may have been anything but.

The Romans knew the river as Fluminus Meduwaeias, and by the time King Alfred was beating off the Danes from Rochester in 886 the river had become Medwaeg. In ancient Sussex documents of the thirteenth century it is referred to as Aqua de Medewey, and William Lambarde in his *Perambulation of Kent* (1570) thought the name could mean "middle", "midway" or even "midday". His final idea was: "because of the fruitful medowe that maketh all along the course of same".

That, then, is the name; the next thing is to find the source, and as with more famous and longer rivers where they rise has often been in doubt. Nevertheless, we can say quite definitely that the source headstream rises from a spring in the Tunbridge Wells Sandstone of the Wealden rocks near Ashdown Forest not far from the village of Turners Hill (now in West Sussex). However, there are four principal headwaters, each with a number of tributary rivulets, and three of them at one time or another have been described as *the* source headstream, and I have walked all four to try and find the exact source. After much enquiry the Ordnance Survey informed me that the river Medway rises south of Miswell Wood and was the opinion of the Kent River Board's Divisional Engineer that it was the source of the river Medway. If you want to see it clearly on a large map or plan you will have to consult the 1:2500 sheet TQ 3335.

The actual spot is marshy and overgrown with the infant stream spouting forth unromantically from a kind of drainpipe which, if you are really determined to see it, can be reached from the village by going down the hill towards Crawley Down on the B2028 to a bridge at the bottom.

The stream flows parallel with a line of electricity pylons—part of the wood was cleared for it—and by walking up the edge of the wood suitably clad and with wellingtons you may bend down amid the mosses, brambles and bracken and gaze upon the trickle that 70 miles (112 kilometres) later, with the help of the Thames, will flow into the North Sea.

A tributary brook on the right bank may tempt you to follow it up the hill to Butcher's Wood. Here you will find a small cemented basin from which a spring wells up. This was beautifully described by Donald Maxwell in his *Unknown Sussex*, and referred to later by Robert Goodsall in his book on the Medway. Alas, this is not the source, although many of the locals will stoutly assert that it is.

Nowadays this source region, lovely as it still appears, is not quite the isolated Sussex that Maxwell knew, or even the "enchanting area of East Sussex" of Goodsall. The motor-car and housing estates have seen to that (and also meanwhile it has become West Sussex) but there is still much to look at in this corner of typical High Weald ridge-and-vale country, and plenty of not quite so well-known history in its background.

Miswell Wood is named from meas or moss, and one can imagine it as being part of the great Silva Anderida of the Romans or the later Andredsweald of the Saxons. Modern research has revealed that the South Saxons were earlier in clearing and colonizing the Sussex Weald than was once thought, and this tract of land around the Medway headwaters lay in an area of their pioneer farming. They divided it into virgates (an old land measurement) of about 100 to 150 acres, but it still had much rough uncleared land.

Turners Hill nearby, now rather undistinguished, gets its name from the family of Galfridus de Turnur and was an important village on the old coaching road from London to Brighton. William Cobbett talks about it thus: ". . . on the road from the Wen [his derogatory name for London] to Brighton, through Godstone and over Turner's Hill . . . which is the pleasantest coach road from the Wen to Brighton."

The village was much connected at one time with the Cowdray family at Worth further along the B2110 road, and had its fair quota of pubs, three at one time, called the "Lion", "Unicorn" and "Crown". An earlier Sussex writer mentions that the old farmers meeting in these hostelries had some pretty strange "cures" for the perennial complaints of the last century. For hard skin you plunged your feet into cow dung and stout mixed, and a frightful drink of castor oil and vinegar was recommended to cure asthma.

Unfortunately the village is rather overblown with modern housing. However, I met one very cheerful modern inhabitant, Mr O'Donoghue, who had arrived by way of Carshalton and Crawley and who lived in an old house; he was planting his potatoes when I talked with him and he was full of interesting local information, having taken much trouble to find out about his surroundings.

Talking about Sussex potatoes, it is surprising to discover how rare they once were in the county. An old yeoman of Horsted Keynes (just south of Turners Hill), William Warnett, recalled that potatoes had never been heard of before 1765 in the neighbourhood, but in that year Lord Sheffield brought some back from Ireland, although no one knew how to plant them. At length someone managed to plant them on Lady Day, but for a long time there was much prejudice against potatoes and they were linked with religious fervour, "no Popery, no potatoes" being a popular cry.

Before going off downstream with the headwaters a diversion along the B2110 merits one Michelin star for interest. Soon you will come to Worth Abbey, a group of buildings with fine wide open vistas over the Sussex Weald. Conspicuous is a mock Tudor mansion, formerly called Paddockhurst, which was built in the spacious 1870s by Anthony Salvin and later acquired by Lord Cowdray.

A longer detour worth two Michelin stars (at least) is to continue down the old Brighton coach road to Selsfield, a name meaning open land. Near to this breezy ridge, thoughtfully bought by the National Trust as early as 1912, is the line of the old Roman road—London to Portslade Way—carefully traced out by the late Ivan Margary (*Roman Ways in the Weald*). From this ridge far to the horizon an alignment was laid out by Roman engineers to Clayton on the distant South Downs nearly 2,000 years ago. It is incredible to think that these Romans' ability as roadmakers, heating and sanitary engineers has only just been equalled in the twentieth century. The road's purpose was to connect the rich corn-growing area of the South Downs (realized in our own time for the same land use) with London and the rest of Roman Britain; an evidence of its making is just there off the road to Selsfield Place where an artificial mound (or agger) containing road-metalling shows that the road was 28 feet (over 8½ metres) wide.

Beyond the fork at Selsfield House the road passes through some of the finest ridge-and-vale scenery that we have left in Sussex. These steeply wooded vales with their little streams rise up to massive craggy outcrops of Ardingly sandstone and are at their most impressive in Chiddinglye Wood amongst wide rhododendrons and azaleas. Enormous blocks have become separated from the main sandstone ridge by dark, vertical, almost knife-edged chasms. One of these great blocks, locally famous as Great-upon-Little, is so completely isolated that it overhangs on all sides.

On seeing this spectacular landscape the question at once arises—what caused it? One reason is that during the permafrost periods of the Ice Age, when the climate was like the tundra type in northern Norway today, the thin layer of soft clay would have frozen and later thawed out and flowed down to the valley bottom where it would have been carried away by the swiftly flowing melt-water streams. The more resistant sandstone then remains.

A pleasant climax to this beautiful Wealden landscape is a little further along the road at Wakehurst Place. This is one of the finest and most spacious of the National Trust gardens on a very old estate—the name means Waca's Wood—with an Elizabethan house built in 1590 by Sir Edward Culpeper. He was one of the Sussex branch of an extraordinary family, whose names will recur throughout these pages, being remarkable for their riches and great distinction of their many members in Kent and Sussex.

Later owners of these superb grounds, especially the 1st Lord Wakehurst of Ardingly, embellished them with conifers, rhododendrons and many flowering shrubs. These combine the wilder and natural Sussex Wealden scenery with the best expression of horticulture, and today they are expertly maintained and cared for by the Royal Botanic Gardens of Kew. The 476 acres (192 hectares) are large enough to give solitude amid a blend of natural watery landscape, orderly shrubs and exotics such as the rare Chinese Tea Tree (*Stuartia sinensis*) and the Dove, or Ghost, Tree (*Davidia involucrata*) sometimes called the Handkerchief Tree because of the dense soft white underside of its leaves, which I came across in my wanderings. Completely different is the Rock Walk which is a miniature escarpment of the rocks seen earlier (Ardingly sandstone) grown over with twisted old beeches, yews, rhododendrons and ferns sprinkled with wild flowers.

To return from this foray into wild Sussex you can leave the B2028 and by various paths reach the Philpots Iron Age Camp above Chiddinglye, and go on to West Hoathly. On these heights was the legendary last stand of the Belgae against Caesar during 54–53 B.C., on the evidence of finding agger (to make a quickly built sloping causeway up which the Romans attacked) and pits from which the agger was dug. I came from West Hoathly, failed to find camp or agger, became thoroughly exhausted through continual ascent and descent amongst the sandstone, and was eventually restored with some welcome coffee by kind Dutch ladies working nearby at the Philpots Rudolf Steiner School.

West Hoathly is on an extremely ancient site, being an old hill-top village. The name means heath, indicating a very early South Saxon cleared open space in a frontier area. An old Charter of 765 refers to the "Baere teage" barley clearing at West Hoathly. This means an early church, but it wasn't mentioned in Domesday as the hamlet was attached to a holding in a more settled part of the Sussex Low Weald.

The outside of St Margaret's Church is pleasing, but much rebuilt in many styles; the inside I have not seen, as I was unable to obtain the key, but I believe it contains the remains of a large mysterious oak chest. The church lych-gate, a nice piece of workmanship, was the gift in 1923 of William Robinson, a great gardener whom we shall hear about shortly at Gravetye Manor. The village is full of fine old buildings all quite different from each other; the most ancient is the fourteenth-century Priest's House associated with Anne of Cleves (one of the luckier of Henry VIII's wives and who lived in several fine houses after her divorce) and now an archaeological museum. Another building I liked was the Old Parsonage, a seventeenth-century hung-tiled farmhouse, shop and private house over the years, whose owner very kindly described its history and showed me the exterior. Others certainly worth a look at are Upper Barn and Combers Cottage.

The pub has an interesting name, Cat Inn, derived from the leopards in the arms of the Duchy of Lancaster going back to 1371 when Ashdown Forest was granted to John of Gaunt. Inside are some intriguing oriental prints of cats and a fine worked sampler.

Eastwards from here is a place in such contrast that you could be persuaded you were back in London suburbia. This is the greatly expanded village of Sharpthorne, grown almost in spite of the closure of its station (called West Hoathly) and double-track line, which further south has risen phoenix-like to become the Bluebell Railway.

Which came first, the chicken or the egg? It seems planning pottiness to expand the village and then let B.R. close the station, or expand the village after the station was closed. Either way means a very crowded by-road along which all the commuters roar, cursing people like me who happened to be exploring the area rather precariously on a bicycle!

We must now go back to the infant Medway and its sister headstreams, but before we begin we need to have an outline of the Wealden iron industry. This is because for much of the journey downstream we shall be constantly meeting relics of its long existence.

The pioneer research worker was Ernest Straker who spent much of his life identifying the many sites throughout the Weald. Modern research on the technology of early ironmaking has shown some defects in Straker's work but, in spite of this, his *Wealden Iron* (1931) still remains the most complete work. It was all the more impressive because he was neither an archaeologist nor a metallurgist, and he was often ill—his field work was indeed heroic. The modern research is being carried out by the Wealden Iron Research Group, who actually simulate the early methods of smelting, and later it is hoped to publish a comprehensive survey.

The Wealden industry is ancient, stretching back to the pre-Roman Celtic Iron Age people whose few known sites were dated by coarse pottery found in their slag and refuse heaps. These ancient ironmakers worked on the fringes of the Weald where in the Medway area northwards they supplied only a small domestic market.

By contrast the Roman industry was very extensive, and still more sites are being discovered, especially in Ashdown Forest (as we shall see later). As their sites were so often near their roads it has been suggested that whilst they were making the roads, the Romans actually discovered iron ore near the surface.

Roman ironmaking in the Weald lasted about 200 years and was one of the largest concentrations of industry in the Empire; then it dramatically declined. When a large man-made enterprise suddenly collapses the reasons are often obscure, but it seems that the easily found ore in the Wadhurst Clay at the junction of the Ashdown Sands ran out. Some of this early ore was extraordinarily rich, compared with later workings, having 55 per cent iron content (it was iron carbonate coated with iron oxide: siderite-limonite). Another reason for decline was the deforestation of the primeval forest of oaks, ash and beech, because although they were only using the branchwood for charcoal, they were using it in vast quantities; but there may have been another reason which we shall see shortly.

The early ironworking sites were called bloomeries; and the roasting furnace was a primitive clay-walled mound of iron and charcoal. To get a decent draught was a very tiring process done by hand or foot bellows through tuyères or clay nozzles, and this resulted in a mass of spongy iron or bloom forming on the hearth. This was impure slag and so hard that they used it to metal their roads.

Now what has emerged from modern research is the connection between the iron industry and the Roman fleet, or Classis Britannica. This has always been rather a shadowy force, but its importance in transport and supply (a support role) was vital. Moreover its crews often took part in campaigns—like modern Marines—as when Agricola invaded northern Britain.

Archaeologists now think that for a long time (about A.D 150 to 225) the Roman iron industry was under the control of the fleet—itself subject to the army. The needs of the army were great, such as large amounts of iron for nails used in military timber works and forts, leading later to the two great defensive walls in the north. It is known that veterans from the fleet (vexillum or vexillations) were working on Hadrian's Wall. The archaeological evidence for this fleet activity is interesting. A hoard of over one million nails made from Wealden iron was found at Inchtuthil in Scotland, and considered to have been transported from their base at Dubris (Dover) after being brought by boat from Bodiam on the Rother estuary across Romney Marsh—then a shallow sheet of water. Also a large number of tiles stamped with the fleet emblem, CL BR, have been found at three Roman ironworking sites: two in Sussex, near Wadhurst and Battle and one in Kent near Sissinghurst. These tiles date from the period about A.D. 150–250. (This very brief account is compiled from the *Archaeological Journal*, Vol. 131, 1974; and also from a private conversation with Mr C. F. Tebbutt, archaeologist, at his home in Ashdown Forest. I have omitted the petrological evidence of Fairlight Clay as it is too detailed. But I consider the whole matter so interesting that I am loath to leave it out of the book—this little piece of Roman history deserves to be better known.)

This crude bloomery process went on rather sporadically for over a thousand years until Tudor times, when it was revolutionized by the new indirect method using a blast furnace (a French invention). This produced cast iron which was then forged into wrought iron, and even steel by purifying it. These processes needed water power with separate water wheels to work the bellows and to operate the trip hammer for forging. They were often near each other on the Wealden streams, ideal for damming up into bays or ponds. Abundant timber nearby and the local iron ore completed the enterprise—a nice example of the location of industry.

Although this Wealden industry produced all manner of products like anvils, hammers, plates, pots, skillets and gressets (Sussex utensils for melting fat for rushlights)—and even garden rollers—it was dependent upon the demand for armaments, i.e. cannon, and consequently was very much an up-and-down affair. Its final decline was on account of many reasons: the use of coke as a fuel, demand for timber in other industries such as shipbuilding, and (particularly in Kent) for the clothing trade, brickmaking, hop poles and as charcoal for oast kilns. Generations of schoolchildren have been falsely taught that the deforestation was caused by a shortage of timber due to felling; in fact the charcoal was made from coppice wood often on estates, and in any case oak was rarely used, beech being preferred.

However, there was a great panic in Whitehall with much hurried legislation to preserve timber for the wrong reasons. Ironically the one thing that might have saved the industry came too late. This was navigation on the middle Medway in 1740, for the dreadful roads in the Wealden mud probably finished off the industry more effectively than anything else!

After our long digression we are back at the Medway source once more—not quite like Spenser's "wherein the Nymphes doe bathe . . ."—as it must be confessed that following the headwaters closely is difficult because of the tangled undergrowth of the shrub and field layers of the Sussex woodlands.

From the bridge on the B2028 the stream runs by the wooden palings of a field to some woods with names like Clarkes Field, Warren and Little Nobs. Further downstream is a splendid example of a river gap on a "micro-scale" where the tiny stream carves through a band of harder rock—a foretaste of its intentions through the greensand and the chalk. Beyond in a marshy part of the watercourse there was a riot of colour in May, when I saw it with the purple-pink splash of foxgloves and the deep gold of marsh marigolds above the iron-stained sandstone. Then comes Burleigh Arches Wood where the going is grim because the wood has a shrub layer dominated by brambles and a field layer of serried ranks of nettles.

Clumps of nettles often cover the banks of the upper Medway and its tributaries, for they grow on damp soils rich in nitrogen. And as the river flows commonly through woodland, there is plenty of decaying leaf litter which nettles like, for the plant is greedy for nitrates and once it has water enough to make them it will squeeze out all other plants by its vigorous growth. This is also why they are so common around cow byres and pastures.

You can avoid all this "nettle jungle" by taking a public footpath on the right when you leave Turners Hill on the B2028, leading to a track beyond the wood. Not long after the stream is crossed by the line of the Roman road we saw at Selsfield; Margary says there is a distinct earth agger by the stream, but I'm afraid I didn't find it.

Onward the stream becomes marshy with rushes and glimpses of wildfowl, and suddenly it opens out on to a beautiful view of the lakes of Fen Place Mill. This is a splendidly wild area, but kept for exclusive wild duck shooting and fishing. Walking along the lakeside path I heard a rustle and an adder glided by—proof enough of a true wilderness, for they are in fact timid creatures. Fen Place Mill, the first mill on the Medway, is a pleasant old building. Here the river is joined by the most northerly headwater which rises at Bower Place in Crawley Down—or did, for I fear the source area has become submerged in a mass of building. This stream is best reached from East Grinstead.

The combined waters now flow south-eastwards to the B2110 road, and follow it for a short way to reach a very high railway embankment through which the road is virtually a tunnel, for here the arch portals are the same shape as the old Brighton railway (the L.B.S.C.R.) used for its own tunnels. The Medway burrows under both road and former railway, for alas it is the northerly closed section of the old Bluebell and Primrose Line from East Grinstead to Lewes. This was a well-built line, and Colonel Yolland, a famous Board of Trade Inspector in his day, stated publicly that it had seldom fallen to his lot to inspect a railway that was so thoroughly satisfactory (May 1882). The

present Bluebell Railway is making strenuous attempts to rein-
state the line from Horsted Keynes to East Grinstead but their
first attempt was rejected by the local District Council—in spite
of the County's blessing. They now await a Public Enquiry in
June 1981 (postponed from December 1980) and are "fairly
confident" in their case for Appeal against this "dog-in-the-
manger" decision over which the spirit of Beeching seems to
hover with malignant intent. Ironically, B.R. is quite willing to
co-operate with "run-round" facilities for the locomotives and
an interchange platform at East Grinstead, the Company's Sec-
retary told me when I visited this enterprising little line at
Sheffield Park.

The stream now winds through the garden of a house suitably
named "Medway", belonging to Mr Jones, a retired market
gardener. He told me how the river was first diverted by the old
Brighton Railway in 1882 (there are no details in the original
railway contract, only the mention of the cost of diverted
streams), and again later by his father. The first diversion ran
through the Joneses' land and when Mr Jones's father had built
the present house he diverted the river behind what is now a
splendid rhododendron bush. The old line of the stream can be
clearly seen by a semi-circle of bright green grass.

At Kingscote the Medway is joined by the third headwater
which rises in a pond by the side of the old coach road (B2028) at
Turners Hill and then flows down a picturesque deep valley to
join the main stream. This is incorrectly marked on the 1:25,000
O.S. map as the Medway, and so is yet another false clue.

From Kingscote the small river flows along the edge of woodland at Ridge Hill very close to a Roman bloomery excavated by
Straker in 1927. This was the most northerly outpost of Roman
ironworking in Sussex, and being close to the old Roman road its
output went direct to London.

Not far from here the Medway passes through a large patch of
vegetation where shrubs and waterside plants are growing un-
disturbed to enormous heights—a glimpse of the original Weald
before man, grazing animals and fire altered the natural
growth.

Soon it reaches Mill Place, once the home of an ironmaster but
now a farm. The furnace here was typical of the boom and
recession existence of many ironworks, having worked in 1574,
then declined and been repaired again in 1664; but it had quite a
long life for it was working as late as 1763 when they were
casting the small swivel guns used on ships' bulwarks and in

boats. The underlying Wadhurst Clay ironstone often stains the stream, and if you've sharp eyes you may see cinders in the stream bed.

Behind the farm is the confluence of the fourth headwater from the lake at Gravetye Manor. You can reach this by road from Kingscote, along Vowels Lane and then a long drive through the beautiful woods owned by the Forestry Commission. The name Gravetye comes from *grafta* meaning an enclosure or copse, and the gabled Tudor mansion was built in 1598 by an ironmaster called Richard Infield who married the inevitable Culpeper. This furnace also dated from 1574 and it was said that half the Sussex iron graveslabs were made by Infield. The life of the furnace ended in a great burst of gunfounding and early mortar-bombs known as "bum-shells" (our modern word bombshell) in the 1760s before being finally abandoned in 1787. After that the furnace pond seems to have dried up until the end of the nineteenth century when the manor became the property of William Robinson, the "father of the English Flower Garden". He led a revolt against excessive formality in gardens and for fifty years laboured here to put his ideas into practice, reviving and enlarging the pond and laying out the gardens (which can be seen at certain times), and finally dying at the ripe old age of ninety-six. The manor is now a private hotel, much used by overseas visitors for the lake fishing in spite of aircraft noise from Gatwick. Some of the surrounding oak woodland here is said to be relict oak surviving from the great primeval Wealden forest.

The fourth headwater rises in these woodlands and flows through the lake down past many conifers and—in spring— bluebell-covered banks, to join the parent stream at Mill Place. The Medway, by now a small river, flows under an old arched bridge adjoining a small gauging station and glides beside banks luxuriant with waterside vegetation of the many varieties of the carrot family such as cow parsley, marsh pennywort and whorled caraway. As the river gets bigger, alder trees become more common and the river enters a wide valley. Soon a large and unlikely lake appears, which at first sight seems out of place. This is Weir Wood Reservoir, but the next chapter will tell of its origin and use.

3

Weir Wood, East Grinstead and Forest Row

Before 1951 the river Medway flowed through a broad valley, under Willet's bridge on the East Grinstead road near Weir Wood and past Brambletye to Forest Row. This wide valley with only a small river was probably the result of a geological process called valley bulging caused by permafrost conditions in the Ice Ages. The local Wadhurst Clay thawed out and then flowed down the slopes and was washed away by the fast-flowing river swollen with melt-water.

Crawley New Town, 7 miles (11 kilometres) distant, needed water, and here seemed a suitable site to supply it, and also to store flood water.

Nearly thirty years later this Sussex lake appears to fit quite naturally into the landscape. I say "appears" for although we have become used to these man-made lakes the world over, personally I always find them slightly out of place when they are in gentle, lowland landscapes. The western end is a haunt of waterfowl and interesting aquatic plants, and although the lake is scenic enough with good amenities for fishing, boating and sailing, the walker is rather neglected. I walked around the lake once in early March with a dog, along a narrow muddy footpath severely restricted by a hedge and high railings, well away from the lake shore, which is apparently left for those who fish.

The dam at the eastern end cannot be crossed (officially) by those without a fishing permit, and so a circuit of about 8½ miles (13½ kilometres) had to be completed by judicious trespassing—which incidentally gave much better views from the south side. Fishermen and visitors to the bird sanctuary at Spring Hill have paved roads, a useful convenience for the motorized, but one does wonder whether these outdoor and nature lovers have lost the use of their legs!

Spring Hill Wildfowl Park was ingeniously made out of a 10-acre (4-hectare) garden full of springs that was attached to the 1501 stone farmhouse on Mudbrooks Farm. Conceived at first as a water garden, the ponds were later used for exotic waterfowl—particularly rare specimens like the Hawaiian Ne-Ne geese that Sir Peter Scott saved from extinction. The many species of geese, ducks and swans wander about happily enjoying their ponds at different levels, their varieties of plumage making it seem like a moving flower-garden.

The waters of Weir Wood have closed over the old Admiral's bridge, named from Admiral Lord Seymour, an ambitious man in Tudor times (Henry VIII's brother-in-law) who had tried to marry Elizabeth, Mary, and Anne of Cleves, and in the end married Henry VIII's sixth wife and widow, Catherine Parr. He had been Master of Ordnance and was accused of what in effect was piracy, and was executed in 1549. Partly submerged too is the Roman bloomery identified by its second-century Samian pottery unearthed in 1928 by the persevering Straker at Walesbeech on the southern bank. This is the only ironmaking site in the Weald mentioned in Domesday, where it is described as a "ferraria" in the hundred of East Grinstead. As the Wadhurst clay here is full of ironstone there were other sites along the original river such as Stone Farm furnace, the Standen bloomery and a forge downstream at Brambletye; now all is quiet although at one time the valley must have rung with the sound of hammers in a wild woodland setting.

However, civilization is not far away in the form of Standen Grange, bequeathed to the National Trust in 1972 by Miss Helen Beale, the daughter of its owner, and one of the Trust's few Victorian houses. Built from 1892–4, it is the only surviving important house by Philip Webb, the architect, and was a £12,000 protest against the then architectural standards. The interior was closely associated with William Morris and his famous firm of "art decorators", whose designs of furniture, textiles and wallpaper dominate—as befits a man who had great influence on the renaissance of decorative art. Many objects inside are by other famous sculptors and painters of that era: George Frampton and Alfred Gilbert—who made the statue of Peter Pan in Kensington Gardens and Eros in Piccadilly Circus —as well as Ford Madox Brown and Sir William Nicolson. Notwithstanding all this, for many visitors the overall effect is one of great nostalgia because they will be reminded of their childhood, especially in the bedrooms and again in the grounds with their fine views. This feeling comes because although the house is less than a hundred years old it is redolent of the spacious days, however socially unacceptable they may seem to some nowadays, before plastics, labour-saving gadgets and central heating so altered the domestic scene.

Downstream past the dam at Weir Wood is the confluence of a small stream coming from East Grinstead. You can follow this

back by a footpath to what is still a pleasant town although
heavily and noisily plagued by traffic and with housing estates
shooting forth to all points of the compass. The old town has a
fine High Street and side alleys with many notable buildings
including Clarendon and the Old Stone House once lived in by
judges (now solicitors), a reminder that East Grinstead was an
important assizes town. Many buildings are roofed with Horsham stone, a compact limey sandstone from the Weald clay,
which was at one time much used for paving stones and roofing
slates. It is extremely heavy and must have caused a few roof
beams to creak or crack under its weight; many small, unpre-
tentious houses were also roofed with it and were known locally
as "slab castles". It is pleasantly brownish in colour and usually
covered with mosses and lichens which stick to it like glue.

East Grinstead is on an old site which was a South Saxon
clearing in their Andredsweald: Greenstede, or green place.
Fairlight Farm just outside confirms this as its name also means
a bracken clearing (fearn or fern). By Domesday the hundred
was very large and scattered, with 36 households and 12½
teams of oxen, and extended far to the south-west where West
Grinstead now stands—a village 20 miles (32 kilometres) away.
The town prospered, became a borough and returned two M.P.s,
one more than nowadays with 60,000 electors. Its eighteenth-
century prosperity was such that the local businessmen issued
their own coinage, and like many Sussex towns its church—St
Swithin's—was very early. The structural history of this church
would perhaps make a good building manual of how not to do it,
because in 1785 it fell into ruins as a result of the collapse of the
rebuilt tower that had been struck by lightning in 1683. In
1787 the ruined church was the scene of a romantic wedding, for
the second son of the Earl of Egmont, the Hon Spencer Perceval,
was secretly married to his sister-in-law, Jane Wilson, after
their betrothal had been discouraged, he being then but a brief-
less barrister. Like the town he prospered greatly, but the story
has an unhappy finale, for as Prime Minister he was the only
one (in our history) ever to be assassinated—in the lobby of the
House of Commons.

The church story continues for it was redesigned and rebuilt
with a very high tower—which can be seen for miles—but gave
rise to a cynical comment: "large parish, poor people; large new
church, no steeple". In 1836 a pinnacle blew off in a gale, damaging the nave; later in 1929 the flagstaff fell down damaging
another pinnacle, which later fell through the church roof. By

this time the parishioners had had enough and the pinnacles were shortened. It could be added that this church was truly all things to all men for from 1708 to 1785 the Free Grammar School was in the vestry, and up to 1863 the fire engine was kept at the base of the tower. However, the church contains one very interesting thing: the oldest Wealden iron graveslab dating from 1570. Apparently this was used at one time as the doorstep of the vicar's scullery.

The architectural gem of East Grinstead is Sackville College, built in 1619 by Robert Sackville, 2nd Earl of Dorset, in the form of a square and mainly of Horsham stone, said to have been filched from the ruins of Buckhurst House at Withyam. Still he was clever and economical for it served as a Sackville hunting lodge, as it was halfway between London and their Sussex estates, and also had a set of almshouses, known as the Dorset Lodgings, for thirty-one people and their warden.

I knew these splendid Jacobean buildings well, because for some years I used to visit the College regularly to see my grandmother's old housekeeper who had been a faithful family retainer for thirty-four years, and served the college as a matron for a while. I remember there used to be many fantail pigeons in the quadrangle until they all suddenly forsook the place, as birds and animals sometimes do for no known reason. The funds of the seventeenth-century founder's bequest are now able to support only half of the original number so some of the present flats are rented to outside retired people at realistic rents.

East Grinstead used to be quite a railway centre with four lines converging and two stations at high and low level. The Bluebell and Primrose Line left for Lewes by spanning the Medway tributary with a fine ten-arch brick viaduct at Imberhorne, now high above housing estates. Imberhorne's name meant a corner of land where raspberries grew, from the early English *Hindberie* (raspberry) which still survives in the north as hindberry, and in modern German as *Himbeer*. The other single lines went to Three Bridges (Crawley), and via Forest Row to Tunbridge Wells. You can still walk along the disused Three Bridges route to see the fourth Medway headwater in Rushetts Wood, a very leafy stroll until you come up against the suburban horrors of Crawley Down. These would make any thinking person wonder why planners and builders are allowed to massacre a rural landscape that has been pleasant to behold for centuries. I can already hear the protest, "people must live somewhere". But with all the techniques of the twentieth century need the houses be so stark, ugly, and so *many*?

The surviving double-track line goes northwards to London via Oxted. But the whole layout of East Grinstead's railways has been short-sightedly destroyed in the last decade, and it is difficult to realize that as late as 1961 there were 39 trains a day from the town. Nowadays the new estates pour forth commuter cars adding to the A22 heavy main road traffic, all causing noise, congestion and pollution apparently endured without protest in the "medieval" conditions of this space age.

We will leave the town on a note of Sussex folklore for until recently there was a strong and widespread superstitious fear of snakes, and in 1936 there were public protests at the erection of a large Caduceus (Mercury's wand with two serpents twined round it), on the façade of the newly opened hospital. Many thought it would bring bad luck to the area.

Coming back once more to the confluence near Brambletye, downstream along the Medway there is a curious assemblage of an old moated site and farm buildings from which emerge forlornly the ruins of Brambletye House. Brambletye's name relates to the old English *Bremel teag*, an enclosure marked by brambles. Here is another outpost of the South Saxon forest clearance and a continuously inhabited site over the centuries in a quiet corner of the upper Medway valley.

The original moated house with its adjacent water mills was given to Earl Cola by Edward the Confessor, and later by William I to the Comte de Mortain. They were among the few Wealden water mills mentioned in Domesday as most of the Saxon mills were attached to abbeys or monasteries and there were few of these in the Weald before Norman times. Brambletye is mentioned no doubt on account of the presence of a priest at the manor. The moated house is lost in the mists of time, but a successor, Brambletye House, was built in about 1450 by Richard Lewknor, whose family became M.P.s for East Grinstead. Then in 1574 Robert Reynolds, the ironmaster at Mill Place, had a forge here, but has left no trace except for a little cinder.

In 1631 a Jacobean house was built by Sir Henry Compton; some of the stone—like that of Sackville College—was thought to have come from the ruins of Buckhurst House. Compton's house with its unusual ogee-shaped corner roofed tower had a short inhabited life, because a later tenant, Sir James Richards, was suspected of treason and fled to Spain in 1683. The building became ruinous under rather mysterious circumstances, as later tenants of the estate (Biddulphs) were believed to have used horses to try and destroy the towers, by dislodging stone for building purposes, and ironically the upper part was cannibalized for building. The house was the subject of a romantic novel, *Brambletye House* by Horace Smith, written early in the nineteenth century, which the critics considered a serious rival to Scott's *Waverley*! And thus Brambletye has stood, an empty shell, for close on 300 years.

The present farmhouse, also a seventeenth-century building, has been tastefully restored, though much altered. Through the kind hospitality of the present owner, Mr Brian Hale, I discovered much about the past history of this upper Medway estate, whose owners have included Danish bankers and a whisky distiller. Mr Hale farms some 286 acres (115 hectares) highly efficiently, growing barley and continuous winter wheat. His wife, Mary, is a most successful stockbreeder with a fine Sussex herd, and has won several awards and bred a good bull. This is a very old breed which provided the original oxen that hauled the Wealden cannon through the heavy claylands, and doubtless they were the breed that Daniel Defoe saw in a village near Lewes on his tour of 1724: "an ancient lady, and a lady of very good quality, I assure you, drawn to church in her coach with six oxen . . ." The present breed has a number of proven characteristics that produce good beef cattle, but I was told this about modern beef production: "Lowland suckler beef is the most expensive way of growing beef known to man—nevertheless Sussex cattle decorate the Downs like no others, and if you do them well you'll break even . . ."

Before I left the farm Mr Hale told me frankly that it only pays because he does another job—often working far into the night. This set me thinking—why is modern British farming so expensive? There may be many reasons: high interest rates, expensive mechanized equipment, poor marketing and not least perhaps the British diet that demands expensively produced quality plain food too cheaply.

With all this in mind I set off over the old seventeenth-century bridge that spans the Medway, repaired recently by Mr Hale, and went down the green valley to Forest Row on the slopes of Ashdown Forest.

Forest Row in contrast to the surrounding Wealden villages is a "newcomer"; the name dates from only 1461, and it wasn't even a parish until 1894. The village began from hunting stables and cottages for foresters and huntsmen for the Royal

Forest at Ashdown, hence a "row of houses or cottages". Not so long back it had an interesting local industry, that of making birch brooms, a trade that was carried on by one family named Bennett for over 200 years, even having served Royalty. The raw material was brought to the broomyard from the higher, more heathy, parts of the forest. The village makes one appearance in literature when Conan Doyle's Sherlock Holmes solves the mystery of the "Black Peter" case in 1895, a gruesome mystery of a man found pinned to the wall by a harpoon in a house called Woodman's Lee, with a suspect who stayed at the Brambletye Hotel. Today the village is pleasantly nondescript with a fine pub, the "Swan", far older than the church; but it is clean and tidy having won the best-kept large village award in 1975.

A fair-sized stream called the Kid Brook joins the Medway here, and upstream is the house of Kidbrooke Park. This estate began as an enclosure award in 1693 from Ashdown Forest for deer and gradually evolved into a country gentleman's mansion greatly influenced by the change over the years in transport. Those changes began with the Croydon to East Grinstead turnpike reaching the estate boundary, followed by the Brighton railway which reached almost as far, now superseded by the A22 main Eastbourne road. The Palladian-style house was built over ten years from 1724 by William Neville, who later (and rather unexpectedly) became Lord Abergavenny.

Of the many owners that followed there were two that have left their mark on the house and grounds. The first was Charles Abbott, later Lord Colchester, Speaker of the House of Commons, who asked Humphrey Repton, the landscape architect, to embellish the grounds according to Repton's romantic concept. This was done with cascades, a canal and a series of lakes, and the park was landscaped with the planting of tree belts at a time when there was great interest in the introduction of trees from abroad; here specimens of the Tree of Heaven (*Ailamthus altissima* from North China) and the Tulip Tree (*Liriodendron tulipifera*) were planted. The other was Charles Hambro, the banker, who with his wife in the 1930s made paved gardens, glasshouses for exotic tropical plants, and cleverly used a gill above the valley to make a water garden. That was the end of what might be termed its "spacious days" and after a period of commercial ownership Kidbrooke Park became the Michael Hall School, and some of the land was sold for house building.

Now from Lewes, the county town of East Sussex, I had heard

about a grant-aided scheme by the county and the Countryside Commission who were to plant trees and restore water features and weir in the best spirit of Repton's ideas. Some years before I had seen the house and grounds in a rather run-down condition so I went along to see this renaissance. Alas, the economic crisis must have overtaken this excellent idea for apart from the repair of a culvert and some trees cut down little seems to have happened. The house, it is true, was being refurbished, the roof being in a poor condition, but the chief difference from my last visit was some strange new buildings in the grounds. It will be a pity if the scheme doesn't come to fruition for it seemed to be a move to preserve all that is best in the man-made English landscape of Repton's time.

With these thoughts let us pass on to the beautiful river valley downstream from Forest Row into Kent.

4

Ashdown Forest into Kent

After leaving Forest Row the Medway flows eastwards through a verdant valley that is a delight to the eye and probably one of its most pleasant rural backwaters from the High Weald to the Thames estuary. The serenity of this landscape is preserved by the valley road being well above the river; it was at one time the main road (A264) between Tunbridge Wells and East Grinstead but was mercifully reclassified and demoted to the B2110. Even so, side roads in Sussex today are often busy and noisy, and this one is no exception. However, the road was sited to avoid flooding (for the valley is much silted from past storms) and swings south to avoid Upper Parrock and its hill, so the river route is quieter if you want to walk down it.

The right bank flanks the northern slopes of Ashdown Forest bringing the river much nearer to this wilder region than it was at its source. From the forest come many rushing streams flowing down through deeply wooded ravines and clefts, called locally gills, which join the Medway and make it into a real river. These streams were the foundation of the Tudor iron industry—for water power was the prime mover for their furnaces and forges.

Not far from Forest Row along the valley road and over the river by a bridle path is Ashdown House built in 1795 by the young architect Benjamin Latrobe, and a fine example of the Greek Revival school. This house is significant because Latrobe later went to the U.S.A. and led the Greek revival there by building Baltimore Cathedral, the Philadelphia State Bank and part of the Capitol. The house is now a prep school, and through the kindness of the Headmaster, Mr Williams, I was able to see house and grounds with their magnificent view over the Medway valley and Ashdown Forest. The house is undergoing restoration so the roof wasn't at its best, but the entrance by a circular porch with Ionic columns half recessed into the house is most impressive. Inside, the hallway with double-height space draws the eye above the staircase to a most elegant ceiling, typical of this graceful building, which I felt so pleased to see preserved. It was built for a Mr Trayton-Fuller, and a later inhabitant was J. W. Larkin, the Khedive of Egypt's English agent, one of those Victorians that managed our Imperial affairs so well.

Beyond Ashdown House is Lower Parrock, and by crossing over the river into the water meadows one comes to the site of a very early furnace and forge that had many French iron-workers. The perfected blast furnace first came from Lorraine, and by 1544 there were forty French specialists working in the Weald. The Parrock furnace has quite a history, for at one time it was leased to the widow of an ironfounder called John Bowyer who had earlier supplied Henry VIII with "gunstones", as the early iron cannon balls were called (the originals were actually made of stone). The widow, Denise, had been evicted with her workmen from the site by William Saunders who claimed it through a Chancery suit. But Denise was evidently made of sterner stuff, and according to Straker, "rallied her forces and with 18 men armed with staves, bills, bows and arrows, made a counter attack". This she led personally shouting "Down with Greybeard!" (Saunders). The aftermath of this affair is not known, but ironworking seems to have been a risky business in its earlier days. The forge and furnace were idle by 1664, but their closure seems more likely due to the Medway rather than the uncertain economics of war because the site was often flooded by the river.

Soon along this green valley above patches of woodland is Hartfield, but just before the village the river flows by a mel-lowed old wall alongside the fields of Chartner's Farm in which lay one of the pioneer Tudor ironworking sites. This was where the husband of our early "women's lib" fighter, Denise, worked; her son was to become an important ironmaster for Queen Elizabeth at Newbridge, as we shall see later.

Hartfield is another ancient Wealden settlement whose name means open land, where herots—harts or stags—grazed. The connection with hunting is preserved in one of the village pubs, the "Roebuck". And it seems that even 900 years ago it was a well-established village—larger than East Grinstead—for Domesday records 31 households and 18½ ploughing teams. Today the village is a pleasant cluster of weather-boarded houses, pubs and a tall attractive church (St Mary's) built of warm multi-coloured sandstone, with the churchyard lych-gate underneath a very old (1521) stone cottage. Everywhere looks shipshape, but it's a pity the new council estate was sited to overshadow the nice little hill which was a motte and bailey overlooking the river.

The patches of woodland, including some of the "shaws", or hedges, below the village, are very old and were there in Elizabeth's reign for they were surveyed in 1597 by Thomas Sackville, Lord Buckhurst. This was a pioneer survey using the new instruments, theodolite and plane table, to make a map at 16 inches to the mile. Many of the clumps of woodland and fields on the fringes of Ashdown have had little change in well over 500 years.

You can reach Hartfield by the B2110 through a small linear hamlet called Gallipot Street which has a very ancient restored pub called the Gallipot Inn. This unusual name referred to small pots of ointment brought from the Mediterranean in galleys and used by apothecaries (although some say it was honey!)

Down the B2026 Edenbridge road from Hartfield, the Cansiron stream comes into the Medway from its source at East Grinstead. This typical little Wealden stream flows serenely through farmland today with scant evidence of past activity, but north of Great Cansiron Farm is the site of a large Roman bloomery recently revealed by the Wealden Iron Research Group. On what amounts to an almost "industrial area" of 4 acres (1.6 hectares) they collected building materials, coarse and Samian pottery, and it is thought that the ironworkers were a large "private enterprise" group exploiting the ore that had been discovered during the course of roadbuilding nearby.

Before we go off to see the road, north of here on the other side of the stream and surrounded by woodland lies the appropriately named house of Hammerwood. This was the first of Benjamin Latrobe's houses, a large building in three parts in the form of a large central and two smaller flanking pavilions with Doric pilasters and columns in a superb setting of Sussex woods. The interior was spoilt by conversion into flats and the whole lay empty and forlorn when I saw it, its preservation undecided— although to destroy it would be an act of architectural vandalism.

Downstream from Great Cansiron a path leads to a point south of Holyte Common where there is a preserved section of the Roman road known as the London–Lewes Way (traced by I. D. Margary) metalled with iron slag—probably from the Cansiron site. I saw it on a showery October afternoon and as I stood among the Sussex woods my mind went back in imagination nearly 2,000 years. The forest would have been thick and little disturbed except for the iron mining, but the road would have been busy with carts taking crude iron in both directions: London one way, the coast the other. Not far off would be the clang of hammers, and going nearer perhaps one would have heard the odd curse and occasional jokes in bad Latin mixed with Celtic British speech.

However, all is quiet now and further down the Cansiron stream flows near the remains of Bolebrook, a fifteenth-century house of which the great brick gateway with its "onion" cupolas is a most impressive fragment of what must have once been a fine building.

Back along the Medway towards Summerford Farm the riverside in high summer is rich with flowering waterside plants dominated by the very tall Himalayan Balsam (*Impatiens glandulifera*) with its large purple-pink flowers. This is really a garden plant that in recent years has escaped to flourish in river valleys, but it is a bright splash of colour to contrast with the yellow coltsfoot on the rough ground near the river.

At this point a large tributary enters the main river; this, amongst its other names, is the Steel Forge river which rises over 10 miles (16 kilometres) away near Chelwood Gate in Ashdown Forest. The source of this river is in the Isle of Thorns, a patchwork of old (1564) forest enclosures surrounded by rough open common-land; the name goes back to medieval times when it was a stretch of blackthorn woodland.

Today Ashdown Forest is a remnant of the ancient great Silva Anderida wilderness and is the water parting of southern England which is gradually being pushed southwards by the river Medway and its tributaries. This region has always been remote from the Weald proper partly on account of its geology—as this surviving natural wilderness is largely sterile dry acid sands. For all that, it has had a thousand years of mixed history, being used by royal hunters, graziers, ironworkers, squatters, small farmers, commoners and enclosure awards to landowners. It didn't attract Cobbett, for he described it as: "a heath, with here and there a few birch scrubs upon it, verily the most villainously ugly spot I ever saw in England". Today it has shrunk to 6,400 acres (2,600 hectares) and is cared for by a Board of Conservators who have many problems, not the least being heath fires which spread rapidly.

The Steel Forge stream bends towards Nutley, and here at the southernmost outpost of the Medway a look at Nutley Mill is worth a one-star deviation. This is a restored Black Post mill with a tailpole, and was an early type for grinding corn. It was so well restored by the Nutley Preservation Society that they won an Architectural Heritage award in 1975.

The river valley now passes through a part of Ashdown Forest where recent archaeological field work has revealed many Roman bloomeries. We now know that these Roman ironworks were on a very large scale, much more so than previously imagined and (in spite of crude smelting) produced many thousands of tons of iron.

Most of the upper Steel Forge river is in Pippingford Park, a large tract of land that has had a long and varied history from Upper Palaeolithic times to the present day. The name, a Saxon personal one, meant Pippa's enclosure—so it has been cleared land for a millennium. The estate began in the Restoration period when William Newnham bought it and enclosed it with trees as coverts for black grouse. In 1693 the Enclosure Commissioners, after there had been much squabbling about land in the forest, made it their biggest award (2,000 acres or 800 hectares). It has changed hands many times since and the last buyer (in 1918) was a merchant banker from China; his son, Alan Morriss, an airline pilot and keen naturalist, very kindly took me round his grounds.

The river valley here has a chain of lakes used for fishing, with the largest, or Lower Lake, being dry. We walked across the lake bed to see the remains of the dam, or bay, which had been part of the pioneer furnace and forge built about 1500: "3 bow shots above Newbridge". Its history is rather obscure; all ironworking had finished by 1690, when the land thereabouts was described as "good for little else except for growing rabbits". The soil is just that, being a fair example of the sterile Ashdown sands and pebble beds. The dam survived until 1946 when the Army, who still lease part of the area, rather clumsily destroyed most of the dam in their efforts to fish by explosives, no doubt to vary a rather dull diet. Alan Morriss is undaunted and hopes to restore lake and dam, but realizes it will be very hard and expensive work.

On the way back we picked up Upper Palaeolithic arrowheads and worked flints left behind by nomadic hunters following the river when tracking beaver—they were from the North Downs, the flints of course being from the chalk. Standing there in this remote spot in the sunshine in modern England, somehow it wasn't so hard to visualize it all and for a fleeting moment pre-history came to life. The spell was suddenly broken, for far from any vegetation I saw, coiled in the sun, an adder—a little surprising for it was only mid-April, but this is a deep and sheltered valley.

Alan Morriss showed no fear but picked up the snake and showed me the poison sacs, illustrating the difference between the two main types of venomous snakes: the viperine (vipers and adders) and those of the colubrine (or cobra type) whose venom is contained in hollow teeth—far more dangerous. Here maybe lies the basis of the old Sussex legendary distrust of snakes because large numbers of adders are found in Ashdown Forest every year.

Pippingford House, the estate mansion, has a rather curious and complex history, and the earliest house was destroyed by fire in 1836. The story runs that it happened during the butler's wedding celebrations, and as it was 5th November nobody thought it odd to see a far-off blaze burning merrily. The present house, now much modified, was designed by a French architect, Hector Horeau. He was the winner of the design for the Great Exhibition of 1851, but chauvinism prevailed, and the award went to Joseph Paxton (whom we shall come across later).

Later owners seem to have all been interested in preserving wildlife, but—apparently—they were thwarted by their game-keepers. For example, a Captain Banbury tried to re-establish ravens in Pippingford woods, but they were tragically shot "in error"; the name survives in Ravenswood. Another owner, a timber speculator called Anderson, had ospreys, but the last survivor was shot in 1914 for taking trout from the Lower Lake, a not unnatural food for these rare birds, as they are fine fishers. Alan Morriss, too, wants to make Pippingford a wildlife nature reserve, especially for birds of prey such as buzzards and owls, and also for ravens, and he has hopes of re-introducing the beaver. His reputation for tending sick birds of prey and owls is well known locally, and whilst we were in the fields he whistled and a buzzard swept down seizing his offering of a dead day-old chick. The woods near the river are the haunt of heron and kingfisher, which explained the loss earlier that day of goldfish out of my hostess's pond at Nutley. As she is a keen ornithologist her complaints were largely academic.

Two other Roman bloomeries have been excavated on tribu-taries of the Steel Forge river: Stickeridge Gill and Stony Brook by the Research Group. This followed the discovery in 1968 of a late Iron Age hill fort at Garden Hill, west of the Steel Forge river, by Mr C. F. Tebutt, an archaeologist of the group. Later they excavated a small but complete second-century Romano-British bath building, and more recently evidence showed that this hill-top site has had a long succession of occupation by Neolithic, Bronze Age and early pre-Roman Iron Age people. Garden Hill is thought to have been a kind of Roman industrial H.Q., as the ironworking there was on a small domestic scale.

All these exciting discoveries, it would seem, are gradually giving a much clearer picture of Roman industrial activities in Britain. I sought out Mr Tebutt in his rebuilt Wealden stone cottage called the Pheasantry, remote and well within the forest itself, a good place to live for an archaeologist and naturalist. Whilst sitting there talking with him and his wife I had a glimpse of the untiring efforts being made by local landowners to keep unchanged the real nature of Ashdown Forest. A vixen evidently feeding her cubs came boldly into the garden and circled round the bird-table eyeing a large bone; she was there for a long time before making off.

Some time before I had met an earlier inhabitant of the Pheasantry, when it had just been a cottage. This was a remarkable old lady called Mrs Woodhams, who lived there for forty-five years and gave me a vision of what life used to be like in the Forest and the High Weald of the more recent past. Mr and Mrs Woodhams farmed a forestry smallholding of 30 acres (12 hectares) which was mainly heather for thatching, and cutting and selling birch faggots for the broomyard at Forest Row. This was a remote, little-changing but obviously satisfying life in spite of the snowfall hazards of 1947 and 1963 when they were completely cut off. That meant a 6-mile (9½ kilometre) hike in the snow from Hartfield station, as the buses were snowed up but the trains along the Medway valley still ran. Getting to the cottage from the road even in normal darkness was sometimes awkward, with her husband lighting matches to try and find the entrance, but the horse knew and stopped opposite it.

She talked to me at her home in the estate lodge next door to Ashdown Park, a large mansion built in 1867 which had many owners, but the most popular were the Sisters of Notre Dame de Namur, a French order that migrated to Belgium in the nineteenth century and has since become world-wide. The Sisters built their own church in 1920 and set up a local school for all, and were great benefactors to the Forest community before, sadly, financial reasons forced them to leave in 1967.

The modern opening-up of the forest to the car-borne public has posed great problems and it is interesting that an old forest inhabitant like Mrs Woodhams and a planning officer at Lewes have identical opinions on this. In short it means quite simply restriction, for there cannot be complete freedom for the urban motorized population to roam at will, however irksome and "inconvenient" it might be to them, for at times they are so ill-disciplined that any real "freedom" vanishes. Anyone who has ever been in a car-free town, like Zermatt in Switzerland, will know the sense of relief this brings. There may have to be many more Zermatts in Europe in future, if life is to be worthwhile.

Further downstream on the Steel Forge river is Newbridge, the most historic blast furnace site in the Weald, for here water power was first applied in England in 1496 to smelt iron ore to make cannon balls. By 1650 this pioneer furnace was abandoned and as was usual became a mill. Sir Henry Bowyer, the son of the militant Denise, was ironmaster here but at his other works he was ironmaster to Queen Elizabeth; relationships with Royalty for ironmasters were often close.

We now come to Cotchford where a small wooden bridge has achieved notice as "Poohsticks Bridge", for not far away is Cotchford Farm, for many years the home of A. A. Milne who wrote the evergreen books of *Winnie the Pooh* and *The House at Pooh Corner*. Many grown-up children will remember that Owl lived in the 100-acre wood (marked on O.S. maps as 500–acre wood), and that Pooh invented a new game called Poohsticks. This game is intimately bound up with the Steel Forge river, which Milne (and his son) knew so well. Both are delightfully described in "Winnie the Pooh" where Pooh's companions— Piglet, Rabbit and Roo—drop their sticks into the river and rush to the other side of the bridge to see whose emerged first.

From Cotchford the more energetic can reach Withyham by a footpath, part of the 81-mile (130-kilometre) route of the Weald-way from Gravesend to Eastbourne—a recently marked out long-distance footpath.

The hamlet of Withyham with its church on a little hill overlooking a small lake makes a most charming and delightful sight—the vision of the homesick traveller returning from overseas, which alas almost never exists in reality.

The church and village are closely tied to the Sackville family, who were Normans from Sauqueville near Dieppe, and even earlier were of Danish origin. The family lived here for many centuries as Earls and Dukes of Dorset at Buckhurst House before finally moving to Knole in Kent about 1603. As we have seen, much of Buckhurst's ancient stonework was cannibalized and this probably began its decay and ruin. Now all that remains of a proud old family mansion which had six towers is a single one standing on such firm foundations of solid masonry that a later tenant trying to use it for road repair on the estate gave up in despair.

At Fisher's Gate further along, one of the ancient entrances to the medieval deer park, a more recent Lord Buckhurst created a model farm on poor soil—an impossible task today with the cost of labour and capital. Withyham's name comes from Wipig (osier willow) and hamm (river meadow) or piece of valley bottom land, especially where it broadens out at a confluence. Here at Withyham was the willow-covered Medway/Steel Forge confluence. The church, as one would expect, is on an ancient site, but the building dates only from 1672, because in 1663 the old church was almost destroyed by lightning—no lightning conductors and plenty of timber. Its interior is dominated by the Sackville Chapel above the family vault; the railings are of local iron, and all around are Dorset and De la Warr memorials and monuments down to the small dignified plaque of Vita Sackville-West, the novelist who died in 1962. I found the most inspiring part of the church was the beautiful Lady Chapel with the Italian altar-piece and paintings from the fourteenth and fifteenth centuries.

Below the road a stream joins the Steel Forge river which has come from Crowborough Warren 5 miles (8 kilometres) away and flows as a pretty watercourse through Buckhurst Park to the De la Warr family house which looks like a typical Tudor residence but isn't, being built in 1738. The grounds were laid out by Humphrey Repton with fine hornbeams leading to the lake which he adapted from the furnace pond of Stonelands ironworks owned by the Earl of Dorset. I wonder what the later landscape gardeners would have done without all these convenient ponds left behind as relics of early water power. The De la Warr family always celebrated their birthdays by firing a private battery of fourteen guns across the lake, but the children who used it for target practice were rather erratic and after a cannon ball had landed in Hartfield the custom abruptly ceased.

Behind the Dorset Arms Inn in Buckhurst Park is a superb spacious cricket field surrounded by trees. Those people who have played the village game, as I did for a while in Sussex, will know that to play on a ground such as this evokes sentiments that no other game can achieve.

After these forest excursions we go back to the Medway beyond Summerford, where it bends northwards near Hale Court and adds to its waters two large tributaries forming a little

Haxted Mill, Surrey, a working museum on the river Eden

The Medway Flood Relief Scheme, Haysden, May 1979. This part of the river will disappear when the scheme is completed

The Great Flood at Tonbridge in September 1968

Maylen Wharf, Tonbridge, October 1980

Lansdowne Square, Tunbridge Wells. Decimus Burton "reborn"

Flooding at East Lock, Barnes Street, in February 1974

triangular area of watercourses bordered by a high railway embankment to the east. One of them is the Hamsell stream, whose distant headwaters have gathered up the many brooks from Crowborough Beacon, Castle Hill and Rotherfield and Eridge Park. Near the source of the Hamsell itself is a farm called "Medway" but its name, I discovered, is recent because the owner, Colonel Adams, a retired farmer from Yorkshire, told me it was originally Catts Farm, from Catts Hill.

Rotherfield in the midst of all this water is a very old site whose name comes from the old word for cattle (hryther) combined with the word "feld", meaning open land for cattle. This became a Royal estate under Alfred with an ancient church, St Denys built in 792, connected with the Abbey of St Denis, near Paris founded in 626. The many small settlements along the Medway tributaries are actually older than Rotherfield itself, whose most famous inhabitant in recent years has been Maurice Tate, an evergreen Sussex bowler.who kept a pub here.

In sharp contrast to Rotherfield is Crowborough, a great sprawling mass of formless modern buildings which is almost suburbia in limbo. Sir Arthur Conan Doyle lived here at Windelsham Manor for twenty years until he died in 1930; he was a dedicated spiritualist, and since 1968 the local people have regarded the house as haunted because in that year the manageress of the property (a retired gentlefolk's home) sensed an extraordinary atmosphere. It has now become an hotel.

At Eridge (the name here means "place of eagles", from *earn*, eagle) by the station from which at one time there was a delightful branch to Hailsham called the Cuckoo Line, the Hamsell stream is joined by one from Eridge Park, the seat of the Nevill family, whose large and beautiful ornamental lake is yet another landscaped ex-furnace pond from an ironworks owned by a former Lord Abergavenny in 1574. The De la Warr custom of firing guns on high days and holidays seems to have been adopted by the locals in Eridge because for many years on holidays and fair days they saved up their money to buy gunpowder to fire an ancient mortar kept on Eridge Green. The local pub here is called "The Nevill Crest and Gun".

The Hamsell stream follows the railway line from Eridge to Ashurst, but on the way at Birchden near the level crossing there are two fine oast kilns—a hint of Kent to come—and Forge Farm, a nice Wealden cottage; nearby is the old spillway down which the stream rushes in flood, making a spectacular waterfall. Behind Birchden, rising up to steeply wooded slopes are the vertical crags of Harrison's Rocks formed of great blocks of Tunbridge Wells Sandstone with wide joints and undercutting. They are a favourite haunt of climbers practising, and beginners learning, the different holds and techniques of scaling vertical or overhanging rocks. Some years ago I was one of them, and whilst near the top ledge I paused to get my breath back and have a good view of a passing steam train; alas! I lost my strength, nerves and impetus and had to be ignominiously hauled by rope to the summit.

Just before Groombridge, south of the base of the triangle of railway lines, this same sandstone forms very rocky outcrops in a region through which a stream flows in a very narrow wooded valley. These have been used to landscape some remarkably fine houses. The most remote near the head of the valley, a seventeenth-century building, was originally owned by an ancestor of mine, William Penn the Quaker, son of the great Admiral Penn, and through marriage he acquired the house now known as "Penns in the Rocks". William Penn's career was a notable one, founding Pennsylvania largely through his religious principles, taking 200 people from Sussex. Ironically, he who had refused to remove his hat in the presence of Charles I (whereupon Charles politely removed his) now became friendly with James II and was suspected of Romish tendencies! After several owners the house now belongs to Lord Gibson, Chairman of the National Trust, who opens these attractive rocky gardens to the public in the summer.

Further down the valley are two very large Gothic mansions built by the architect Norman Shaw in the decade after 1860, in his "Old English Style". They were to provide for Victorian businessmen what was then described as "an escape from the counting house to the country". The escape route was "a short walk to Cannon Street Station, half an hour by train [surely it must have taken longer?], a quick drive in the pony and trap and the soot of London was exchanged for the Sussex pines".

At present there is a great contrast between the two buildings. The first, "Glen Andred", built in 1867, still exists but is now in two parts and surrounded by vast neglected greenhouses and overgrown vines. The other, "Leyswood", was largely demolished in 1950 following damage by its wartime occupiers, but the surviving battlemented gatehouse tower with the tall chimneys and dormers of its adjacent building have been tastefully converted into offices and a residence. The owner, Mr Simpson, who with his son runs a family landscaping business, very kindly showed me over the entire building. This portion is all that remains of a once vast residence that was the home of Shaw's cousin, Temple, a shipping magnate of the White Star Line, as was Shaw's brother, a founder of the Shaw, Savill & Albion Line. But what is left is preserved in the style and spirit of Shaw, and so are the still splendid landscaped grounds above which was once perched a fantastic gazebo. We shall meet more of Shaw's work in Kent.

The valley hamlet is called Motts Mill after a long departed corn mill, and was mentioned to me by Mrs Woodhams of Ashdown, who as a girl lived at Lealands near Groombridge. One of her girlhood joys was being driven to Dane Hill and back in the horse-drawn laundry van from Motts Mill; the laundry there was a mainstay of local employment. This underlies the fact that although these fringes of Ashdown Forest form a beautiful landscape, the soil is poor and infertile and there must have been some rural poverty in earlier years.

Groombridge is our last village in Sussex, and is in two parts, a nineteenth-century Sussex growth and a much more attractive hamlet over the border in Kent with a triangle of green, old houses and a pub. However, before leaving Sussex look at the pleasant 1871 "new" schools built by Norman Shaw.

Over the border are three very fine buildings all well worth seeing for many different reasons. The first, Court Lodge, a little way up the Ashurst road, is the most unusual, for it is really a fifteenth-century Sussex manor house built round a courtyard next to the church at Udimore near Rye. After 1690 it gradually became derelict and was threatened with demolition until the rector, also an artist, called Lawson-Wood, bought it. However, the owner refused to part with the freehold so Lawson-Wood moved the house in 1909 in pieces to Groombridge, by using horse-drawn wagons and traction engines to haul the heavy timbers. It took four years to rebuild, and has been well cared for since; the result can be seen from the outside and the gardens, which are superb, can be visited. Their chief glories are lawns, some fine oaks and a blue cedar with a pond of red water lilies and a mineral-water well that might have turned the village into a miniature Tunbridge Wells.

The second house is Burrswood, built in 1831–8 by Decimus Burton, the architect of Tunbridge Wells and the last great builder in the Greek Revival style. The chief interest of Burrswood now is as a centre for faith healing founded by the late Dorothy Kerin, an Anglican mystic and one of the few known

Anglicans to have borne the stigmata. She had a very beautiful church (Christ, the Healer) built next to the house in 1960, the first Anglican church to be built for healing. The interior is breath-taking with many interesting old church objects brought from all over Europe including pictures, tapestry, crucifix, lectern, candelabra and a seventeenth-century Florentine altar. The house, church and grounds are in immaculate condition and order, with remarkably fine views over the Medway valley.

Groombridge's name is mysterious, for it is a compound of two Middle English words: *grome* (boy or servant) and *brycg* (bridge), but the origin is unknown. Flowing through the village is a stream called variously Hungershall (from Hungershall Park in Tunbridge Wells) or if you prefer it, river Groom, which tumbles down from the High Rocks and flows through Groombridge Place: a mill on it at one time diverted the waters so that a fragment of Kent passed to Sussex.

Groombridge Place, our third house, is a small, perfect Restoration building with a medieval moat and a beautiful fifteenth-century grey stone walled garden. The site is old and it would not be difficult to imagine that the moat once surrounded a fortified house; at all events the previous house had been the seat of the Waller family for about 200 years. John Evelyn, the diarist, described this in 1652 as a "pretty melancholy seat". There is nothing melancholy about the present house built by Philip Packer in 1660, some writers having even seen it as a shy, reticent and modest building. Its charm, I think, lies in its compact simplicity which sets off the slender chimneys and dormer windows and its entrance with the Ionic portico. You can walk close to it and the lake by footpaths, and on rare occasions the grounds are open and even when I visited them on a typical rain-soaked July day they looked good with Wellingtonias, Scotch pines and the splendid rural outlook at the back across the fields.

Below the confluence at Hale Court the Medway acts as the county boundary between Kent and Sussex for about 2½ miles to beyond Ashurst and the confluence of the Kent Water. The Sussex county boundaries in the Weald here with Kent and Surrey are far north of the Ouse–Medway watershed which is a result of the early South Saxon penetration and settlement far beyond the Medway headwaters, and thus give a Kentish river a true Sussex flavour. And so to Ashurst either along the footpath above the railway or by a pleasant river walk along the levée, and we are into Kent.

Part II

KENT—THE MIDDLE RIVER

5

The Surrey Fringes and Ashurst to Tonbridge

The Medway on arriving at Ashurst, the most westerly outpost of Kent on the Medway, passes below the station through the sluice gates of a large mill built in 1792. This was a very fine building with four pairs of wheat stones and a pair of hog corn stones for grinding pig meal—evidently in those days pigs were not just regarded as dustbins for unwanted food. Nearly a century later (1887) it was re-equipped with new machinery and if it hadn't suffered the fate of so many mills—it burnt down in 1930—it might be there now. But it did leave behind a large mill pool which is a favourite spot for anglers and a little island that is ablaze with flowering waterside plants in the summer.

This small village was an important ironworking centre, where we first hear of the Browne family, later to achieve fame or notoriety as the Royal gunfounders. It is difficult to believe that here on the river was a forge and furnace that produced in a few years in later Tudor times nearly 500 tons of ordnance—for all trace is gone now.

Cobbett's description of the village is interesting. In 1823 he followed the Medway valley for many miles, and wrote: "The buildings of Ashurst (which is the first parish in Kent on quitting Sussex) are a mill, an alehouse, a church and about six or seven other houses." Apart from the small station, the place today has hardly changed and, because of its smallness, it is still very pleasing to see, in spite of being now on the A264 main road to East Grinstead. From here it is but a pleasant mile or so to the tributary of the Kent Water, a little river that acts as a county boundary along its entire course beginning with Sussex and Surrey and ending with Kent and Sussex.

There is, however, a far more ancient boundary from here to the sea, for the Medway separated West and East Kent. The name of England's oldest inhabited corner, Kent, is derived from the Celtic root *canto* meaning edge or rim, hence Kantion, the south-east corner. From this came the tribal name Cantii, the Roman Cantium and, at length, Chenth, then finally Kent. Here then is the prehistoric origin of the timeless boundary between the "Men of Kent" and the "Kentish Men" for the river

Medway was the great highway into Kent from the north and divides the county into two natural regions. Later this became the boundary between the Belgae, who were the "Men of Kent", and the Celtic immigrant people west of the river known as the "Kentish Men", and was a very significant and well-marked frontier.

The valley of the Kent Water, which rises on the higher ground to the north of East Grinstead, is secluded, charming, green, woody and not so well known, probably because nearly all the roads cross it. Therefore to see the Kent Water you have to walk it, which is easy enough as paths follow its banks one side or the other.

Just below the source over the border into Surrey is a fine old building surrounded by water gardens called Old Surrey Hall, now divided into expensive flats. Below here the valley and its region is remarkable for the traces of prehistoric man's activity in the form of numerous bloomeries, and just to the north the great Iron Age earthwork of Dry Hill fort in Surrey. Further downstream Cowden was one of the most prosperous and famous Kentish centres of the Tudor iron industry through its reputation for high-quality workmanship. These ironworks are interesting for their connection with a family called Gale. The father, Leonard, was a poor blacksmith from Sevenoaks who became prosperous by long hard work at the Tinsley forge near Crawley. In 1687 Leonard Gale, aware of the profits at Cowden, advised his son to get one of the furnaces there. The son on his father's death in 1690 inherited enough valuable property to buy an estate in 1696 for £9,000—an incredible sum for those days—and later through marriage secured the Cowden furnace at Scarlets and worked it until 1750. This shows how ironworking in southern England could produce self-made men who advanced socially and financially, just as later circumstances in northern England in the nineteenth century had a similar effect. In our own day it seems the breed has disappeared, and Britain is the poorer for it.

Scarlets, the upper Cowden furnace, still has its preserved bay and the large pond is a flourishing fishing area. The lower furnace site at Furnace Farm is now an extremely beautiful lake of 30 acres (12 hectares) made wild and attractive by a great growth of trees and water plants at the top end. Near the road at the lower end is a fine old converted mill house, the inheritor of the furnace in 1786; in the days of its prime the mill was in Kent, whilst the mill wheel was in Sussex! Across the road is a cave in an outcrop of the Ashdown Beds from which the sandstone for the furnace was quarried. It used to be protected by smart wooden palings, but these have been broken down and the cave in this lovely wooded valley is now full of very unlovely refuse.

Cowden village is one of the 477 Kentish places ending in "den", from the Old English "denn", meaning a hollow clearing in the once thick oak forest, originally for pasturing pigs or pannage. A historian called Turley once wrote to the Cowden parson asking if there were other "dens" in his parish. The parson's reply was brief: "Only one," he said, "and that's the parsonage!"

Richard Church thought Cowden was a damp and heavy site, which is no doubt true as the little river can easily flood, but the village is small, compact and pleasant with wooden-fronted houses, and the ironworking tradition lives on through a working blacksmith: Hadlow & Sons. Its tall church has a shingled steeple, and outside by the corner of the east window and north wall are two iron graveslabs dated 1766 and 1772. These products followed naturally from firebacks; the patterns were sometimes interchangeable and they were made in the Weald for 300 years.

After Cowden the Kent Water flows in a verdant, more open valley and joins the Medway, now a true Kentish river, which flows to Chafford. This little waterside hamlet is in a delightful setting, and from the fields along the river bank the small row of houses seems as tranquil a place as one could wish. And if one or two fishermen are sprinkled about the effect is even more peaceful.

A little further downstream are some weirs, where once stood the Fordcombe Paper Mills, yet another fire victim, this time in 1900. Then comes Springhill and right along to Penshurst the river is contained in a basin with a wide valley giving a splendid green vision of the Kentish countryside, whilst the river's course has some striking meanders that are incised or "cut" into the banks. These are quite old geological features as the river here cuts across an upfold, or anticline, in the earth's crust. The meanders were later deepened by the river having to cut down rapidly during the Ice Ages in a period of falling sea level, or land rising, or even a permutation of both. Geology and scenery make a good riverside walk here along the river to a bluff, or cliff, at Nashes, where you can actually see the grey Wadhurst Clay that was so full of the iron nodules or "sows" in the cliff here. If you look in the river bed its colour changes to mottled yellow with grey shaly clay.

Over the footbridge below the cliff brings you to Nashes Farm where by the gate is an old mounting block. These are rare now, but were common enough for centuries as essential conveniences for the mounted travellers struggling through the Wealden mud. Now that we are safely over the county boundary, it used to be said that "Sussex women were long in the leg, because of the struggles they had to pull their feet out of the mud".

Near the river, just over the brow of the hill on our right, is Swaylands, a house built by another Victorian architect, George Devey, whose work and landscaping is very much a part of the Medway valley. Like so many Victorian houses, Swaylands is now a school, which is not the most satisfactory use for a fine house in such rural surroundings. Soon the confluence of the river Eden, the Medway's most important left-bank tributary, comes into view, known locally as the "Point" with a large isolated oak tree in the V of the two rivers. Single oak trees in the middle of fields are often the result of that colourful bird, the jay, hiding acorns and then being unable to find them again.

The river Eden, I find, is a rather confusing river; it was one of Lambarde's four brooks that fed the Medway in his *Perambulations of Kent* (1570) with the source near Crowhurst in Surrey. Upstream from Edenbridge the river divides into four tributary branches: the river Eden itself, the Eden Brook which is much longer, Gibb's Brook and the short Kent Brook. The Geological Memoir for the Sevenoaks and Tonbridge District leaves no doubt about the Medway's attachment to Wealden Surrey for it talks of ". . . the encroachment of the Medway system into Holmsdale (the clay vale that runs from Surrey into Kent) in the west by the Gibbs Brook near Limpsfield."

But we have to go back into Sussex again for the source of the Eden Brook, at its head called the Felbridge Water and only about 3 miles (5 kilometres) from the Medway source itself—but having a rather different journey to where they meet near Penshurst. Along this headwater is a chain of three large ponds —the first in Sussex, the other two in Surrey—all at one time being used for Tudor ironworking. Hedgecourt Pond near Felbridge is a fine sheet of water and worked a corn mill for many years; the last pond is now called Wire Mill which Straker thought looked like the Fens with great beds of Club rush (*Scirpus lacustris*).

It is still a large sheet of water in fine wooded surroundings with its tranquillity occasionally shattered by water skiers practising this sophisticated and exhilarating sport. When I saw the lake they were trying out the water jump, but as they couldn't keep their balance very easily the watchers on the bank (including me) laughed as only those on dry land can when others get very wet. After all these large ponds the Eden Brook flows near that most attractive racecourse of the large village of Lingfield with its two interesting churches—its own large one built in 1431 in the Perpendicular style, and the modern Mormon chapel not far away with a tall spire. It then joins the river Eden south of Haxted in Surrey.

The river Eden rises near Godstone and flows towards Crowhurst Place, a really superb timbered Tudor great house with a moat, that has an unchanging look about it perhaps caused by its rather isolated site in the Surrey Weald some way from the hamlet of Crowhurst. Henry VIII stayed here on his way to see Anne Boleyn at Hever; Crowhurst was presumably a convenient stop on the route from Hampton Court. The village church is approached by a causeway similar to those in the muddy Kentish Weald in the Beult Valley.

Our last place in Surrey is Haxted Water Mill, a very well-preserved fine wooden building with a double mansard roof, because the original was built in 1680, and the other added much later in 1794. This is a most interesting place for not only was it a working mill for 250 years with three pairs of grindstones, and an overshot wheel for 140 years, but since 1969 it has been a working museum. Inside there is an enormous amount to see relating to the world of water mills and water power of the past, one exhibit being the very valuable French burr-stones. These were stones designed to grind the finest flour and were made up of segmented sharp quartz stone bonded by plaster of Paris, and very different from the coarse stones used for meal and feeding stuffs. Fine milling declined rapidly after the arrival of the huge steam-roller mills built in the 1880s near ports for imported wheat, which effectively ended good bread in England. On the upper floor is the unique Wealden Iron Exhibition which shows the recent progress made by archaeologists in revealing the old iron industry, and a huge illuminated map pinpoints the 300 sites.

After all this knowledge I emerged to lean on the parapet of the bridge over the Eden and saw literally dozens of small birds queueing up to bathe in the river on this rare sunny day in July.

From Haxted Mill the river, now made much larger by the Eden Brook, crosses into Kent over the flat Wealden plain past the moated Devil's Den, a peculiar medieval earthwork, to flow under the bridge built in 1813 at Edenbridge town.

This was an important Roman river-crossing which their London to Lewes Way bridged by the Pons Edelmi, and further north of the town at Earlylands I. D. Margary with his painstaking eye for Roman works found Kentish rag metalling 7 inches (18 centimetres) thick, cambered and 18 feet (5½ metres) wide. From this long wide Roman road Edenbridge developed into a linear settlement which later writers either criticized (like Walter Jerrold in 1907 who thought it was unattractive and "scattered along the high road") or praised (like Richard Church who found it in the late 1940s "a pleasant little town"). Well, I saw it in the warm summer of 1947 and agreed with Richard Church, but oh dear! certainly not now. It is a terrible sprawl of "un-architect-designed" housing interlaced with light industry at Marlpit Hill, the whole having burst forth from its linear bonds like a gaping wound.

Only at the fifteenth-century Crown Inn with its sign spanning the road and smuggling history is it worth a pause to stand and stare. Having lived in New Zealand before the days of licensing hours reform, and as a seafarer having experienced the equally uncivilized laws in certain Australian states, not to mention the weird attitude to drink that I found in some Canadian provinces, I can well understand the attraction to the Anglo-Saxon mind of secret drinking of illicit liquor that went on in the tap room of the "Crown".

Edenbridge at one time was a local centre of the boot trade, and one of the traders, Joseph Sparrowhawk, used to walk the 29 miles (47 kilometres) to London and back, taking finished boots and bringing back leather. This tough old walker died in 1898 aged eighty-six.

From Edenbridge the river starts to meander downstream through pleasant water meadows to approach the village of Hever, forever associated with Henry VIII and Anne Boleyn of whom you will be reminded by the Henry VIII Inn. St Peter's Church here used to have the interesting custom of blessing the fields on Rogation Sunday in May, but the tradition has now lapsed for the not very convincing reason of an elderly congregation.

Then comes Hever Castle, and the impossible task of doing adequate justice in describing the building and grounds that so many have done before me. However, a brief historical outline will at least set the scene. Hever began life as a fortified farm-house built by Sir William de Hevre in Edward III's reign, but little remains of it. The present castle was built in 1459 by Sir Geoffrey Bullen, or Boleyn, an ancestor of the ill-fated Anne and a one-time Lord Mayor of London. After the Bullen family disasters in the sixteenth century, and seventeen years of being lived in by divorced wife No 4 (Anne of Cleves) and the haunt-ing of the Eden bridge by the other Anne, the old building decayed through the centuries to become once more a farmhouse.

In 1903 it was saved for the nation by an enlightened Ameri-can citizen, William Waldorf Astor, who restored the old, added the new, landscaped the derelict grounds and diverted the river to make a lake—all with taste, skill, ingenuity and an efficiency that only an American who understood English traditions could display. This work was not carried out without opposition at the time by those who would have left the building to moulder to its unquestioned doom.

Now it is a fine castle with superb grounds, and when seen on a sunny spring day the massed daffodils present a great blaze of yellow-gold. A little later there is the Rhododendron Walk and at all seasons the incredible Italian garden, and behind it the large shimmering lake. Going up the Golden Stairs leading to a walk called the Overlook, stop for a moment to see the anticline, or up-arched fold, of faulted sandstone which is part of the one mentioned earlier at Springhill. Here at least you can see what you might have thought was only geological theory. The grounds were very badly damaged during the disastrous floods of 1968, which was such a fateful year for the Medway valley.

After leaving the lake at Hever the river swings in a loop northwards of the small village of Chiddingstone, which is little more than a short row of old houses typical of the best of Kentish village architecture. For its preservation we are indebted to the National Trust. The row begins with a fifteenth-century half-timbered house, then the Post Office of the same date, then a 1550 house with a wooden porch, followed by Streatfield House of 1572 (the local family and ironmasters) and at the end one of the sixty inns owned by the Trust. This is the Castle Inn, a large sixteenth-century gabled and latticed building, behind which is the Chiding Stone which most people like to see, but has no connection with the village name. It is but a massive boulder of Ardingly sandstone resting on a deeply eroded bedding plane above its base.

The Streatfield family were from yeoman stock who became ironmasters, made a modest fortune and as self-made men were the local "family" and owned Chiddingstone Castle. This building has an extraordinary history beginning as a Tudor house which was pulled down to make a seventeenth-century brick mansion. Another century elapsed and it became a "mock" fortress with towers, turrets and battlements and in the last century came more towers and a Gothic orangery. In 1936 the family died out and in succession the building became a school, was occupied by the Army and finally lived in by a man who would have supported a latter-day Bonnie Prince Charlie had he existed, as he claimed Stuart blood. He surrounded himself with some rather strange objects, amongst which were Japanese armour, Stuart portraits including a nude portrait of Nell Gwynn, and a letter written by the Young Pretender himself.

North of here at Chiddingstone Causeway, near Penshurst Station, are the works of British Cricket Balls Ltd. This title hides a complex history of many firms and traditional Kentish craftsmen, for here in the 1841 factory of Duke and Son are twenty-three craftsmen, all over forty and working in one of the two survivors of hand-made leather cricket-ball makers left in England. The present works had as its ancestor a very old family firm started at Redleaf Hill, Penshurst, in 1760 by a bootmaker called Richard, or John, Duke who subsequently moved to Chiddingstone Causeway. His firm was later joined by craftsmen of the Eade family who had long been making cricket bats further south at Chiddingstone Hoath. This craft was born out of furniture-making in Kent, learnt from woodturning in Surrey, and itself a result of the Sussex agricultural depression of 1815. Later the Duke factory established an informal system of production that would astonish or perhaps rouse the envy of many today. Its basis was piecework to be completed at any time within the fifteen hours that the factory was open. The Duke family were keen on hunting and among their craftsmen were many part-time farmers and publicans. Sometimes at midday the whole lot would go off after an early morning start and have an afternoon hunting, shooting or other business and come back in the evening to complete their tasks by their own oil lamps.

Mr Ken Munday, the present-day firm's Production Manager and himself a craftsman, very kindly showed me round the works where I saw the entire process of the creation of a hand-made cricket ball which is a delightful blend of craft and rural technology. Such processes as stretching and straking the leather, seaming and quilting for the highest grade of balls and stitching with laid saddle stitch went on before my amazed and wondering stare. Craftsmanship of any sort has always fascinated and slightly puzzled me. I suppose the concentration, skill and sheer neatness of it all is beyond the amateur "do-it-yourself" attitude that I possess.

The works contained one or two gadgets of their own invention, for example for stretching the leather—a real "one-off job"—and an interesting phosphor bronze press for enlarging the balls; this came from Crimean War gunmetal! The only other works of this kind is further along the Medway at Teston, which we shall meet later.

From Chiddingstone the river Eden swings in incised meanders, as the Medway does at Springhill, and on the left bank the land rises up to Redleaf Hill where there is a weatherboarded cottage called the "Paddocks" which might be called the eighteenth-century cradle of the cricket ball. Here the Dukes of many generations made cricket balls rather secretly by winding thread around an octagon shaped cork centre called a quilt (hence the process of quilting by quilt winders) and by 1811 were selling them for the high price then of 7/– (35p) each. This was discovered by Joseph Faringdon R.A. who was staying next door with a friend. He was a very famous painter and art connoisseur who shocked his prim, fastidious contemporary, Horace Walpole, by making drawings of all his valuable paintings at his home in Houghton Hall, Norfolk, and then selling the lot to Catherine the Great of Russia for £40,000.

On the right bank of this pretty valley is a hill that rises to a ridge overlooking the river, the southern slopes of which fall away to the distant Medway. Along the ridge, in fine grounds with good views of the two valleys, stands a house called "The Grove", built by Decimus Burton in 1832 and known rather modestly as a sandstone cottage orné. Across the road and sloping down to a small lake is the first Kentish vineyard along the Medway valley, which belongs to "The Grove". The proprietor, Robert Westphal, is a cheerful Australian businessman and apple farmer whose 1978 vintage was certainly one of the best dry white English wines I have tried so far. The bottles are marketed with a very attractive label which reproduces an old print of Penshurst showing distant views of the church and Penshurst Place.

Back along the Medway once more and on the right bank just past the confluence is Penshurst bridge, where the river bank in high summer is a mass of flowering plants, including balsam, cow parsley, sorrel and coltsfoot, with a good view of Penshurst church. Writing not long after the war, Richard Church said that Kent was reputed to be the richest county in all England for its wild flowers, and the richest part was along the Medway valley. One reason could be that the area escaped glaciation, and since the retreat of the ice the climate generally has been warmer and rather more continental than that of other areas. Of course, since Richard Church's time farming has become far less labour-intensive and increasingly dependent upon lethal insecticides and herbicides which effectively destroy bugs and docks but unfortunately finish off butterflies and wild flowers as well. But his premise is still probably largely true as the upper and middle valleys of the river are full of flowering plants.

Now to Penshurst, and it is perhaps best to see the village before you see the great house. The village has some fine Tudor houses, and equally good are the early Victorian Leicester Square cottages built by George Devey. Penshurst is in some ways a memorial to this architect, for he built the pleasant Medway bridge and restored the gardens of Penshurst Place for Lord de l'Isle; he also built the house not far away of Culver Lodge and altered "Culver Hill" for James Nasmyth, the inventor of the steam hammer, who renamed it "Hammerfield". This last house has an interesting history (not always accurately recorded), revealed to me by the kindness of Mr Watney, an engineer who bought the property in 1953 and virtually saved the grounds from dereliction and considerably improved the multi-section house as it had become and which he showed me with some pride. "Hammerfield" was originally the country retreat called "Culver Hill" of F. R. Lee, the eminent landscape painter, and built by him in 1843. Nasmyth retired early at forty-eight in 1856 after his revolutionary mechanical inventions, and provided himself with a 40-foot (12-metre) workshop and an astronomical telescope revolving on a 14-foot (4½-metre) steel ring. He acquired more land and had Joseph Paxton, the designer of the Great Exhibition glasswork which later became the Crystal Palace, lay out the 13-acre (5.3-hectare) grounds as a pleasance with four huge greenhouses and planted Lawson cypress and Douglas fir. The house and grounds are now officially protected, which makes the latest development in Penshurst all the more puzzling. I can record that the Durtnell Garden Estate with its "superior detached residences" has not the approval of the local people and was considerably opposed by them, but to no avail.

Penshurst church, older than either village or the great house, is a mixture and the original thirteenth-century building was by the Penchester family on a Norman foundation. In spite of academic criticisms about church restoration it all seems to blend, as does the rebuilt Sidney chapel in 1820 by the architect (Rebecca) whom Sir John Shelley, the Sidney descendant, employed to resuscitate the time-worn great house.

Now comes Penshurst Place, but its first view ought really to be seen from the north past Redleaf Hill on a cold, clear, bright winter morning. I saw it best thus in mid-February after many earlier visits on crowded hot summer days. This vast and venerable residence is another that defies description, and I suppose its greatest charm must lie in the mixing of styles over the centuries by its great variety of owners. Sir John de Poulteney, another London Lord Mayor, began it with the original fourteenth-century stone house and its superb great hall, followed by the fifteenth-century Royal Dukes, like Bedford who added the Buckingham Building. Then in 1552 came the Sidneys, Sir Henry adding Elizabethan brick and the younger son Robert adding the Long Gallery—his descendant is the present Viscount de l'Isle and Dudley, V.C. The eighteenth century, which everywhere else was so graceful, was desolate here, but the early nineteenth century brought splendour once more as most of the long north front was added in a traditional manner.

The wide sweep of the grounds and park are even older, belonging to the thirteenth-century manorial estate of Sir Stephen de Penchester. Some of the later owners had ideas beyond their purses, for in 1611 when Viscount Lisle wanted to extend his park, his steward demurred as he said it would mean "decaying of so much rent, seeing that you already live in so great and continual wants". And added: "You have alreadye a very fair and sportelyke park as any in this parte of England . . ." The steward's words are as true now as they were then, and adding to its history the indomitable Straker found an ancient bloomery, just north of which is the hamlet of Cinderhill. Over all this lies the spirit of Sir Philip Sidney, born here in 1554 (the house was given to the family by Edward VI in 1552), soldier, poet and courtier, a true man of the Renaissance, who when wounded on the field at Zutphen, in the Netherlands, gave his water-bottle to a dying soldier. He himself was to die after lingering for a month at Arnhem having fought in this rather

useless battle against the army of Philip of Spain, after whom he
was named. Ironically in the famous Spanish infantry *tercios*
were many honourable English Catholic gentlemen. And perhaps appropriately enough one sees many Dutch visitors here in
the summer. But further description is needless; go and see for
yourself the greatest house along the banks of the Medway.

From Penshurst the river flows through tranquil water
meadows with the first Kentish hop-gardens on the right bank
at the bottom of the hill leading to Ashour Wood. Further along
at Ensfield the valley opens out and we are leaving the High
Weald for the Vale of Kent. A neat modern bridge leads to the
village of Leigh (pronounced Lye) with its very large fine village
green; Leigh always seems to have had a good cricket team. The
"big house" here, Hall Place (once called Leigh Hall), is the work
of George Devey and is now owned by Lord Hollenden. Leigh
was an ancient deer park, long ago disparked in the sixteenth
century. The grounds of the house here are often open to the
public, and gardeners will find all the trees and shrubs—
especially the exotics like ginkgo, tulip, magnolia and straw-
berry trees—well labelled, which is not so often done in many
other similar gardens.

After Ensfield the river winds across its plain of gravel terraces and flows under a long six-arched railway bridge that
carries the Tonbridge to Redhill line, which was the original
route to Dover. On the right is the mute evidence of a past effort
to extend navigation to Penshurst, a relic which is now the dry
ditch of the Straight Mile. Beyond this is the vast lagoon of
Hayesden Lake, created from gravel workings and now alive
with sailing craft.

The next bridge over the river is the very long and impressive
pre-stressed concrete viaduct of the A21 Tonbridge by-pass and
immediately downstream the river divides into two channels.
The northern arm was canalized to work an early industrial
undertaking that had a chequered history, originally Ramhurst
Mill, owned at one time by the Lord Chamberlain. The works
became the Powder Mills and for a while were associated with
Sir Humphrey Davy (inventor of the famous lamp, who discovered the electric arc and isolated those curious metals sodium
and potassium) who used them for various experiments and
commercial purposes—but this didn't improve the reputation of
the Cornish genius. The mills were a staple of Tonbridge industry for a long time, even after an explosion in 1916 when pieces
of metal were blown three miles; the mills were later acquired

by I.C.I. and dispersed to Scotland in 1934, and now what's left is a rather dull outpost of light industry.

The main arm of the river continues through an old sluice and weir pool past Barden Park, unites to pass under the main line railway bridge, only to divide once more in flowing through Tonbridge. The northern arm is joined here by the Hilden Brook coming down from the Greensand Ridge via Hildenborough, and a fierce little stream in flood. Hildenborough is rather a dull linear suburban outpost these days, but in Coldharbour Lane there is a house that was at one time called Hollenden Park, whose wartime history was for a while quite exciting for its temporary inhabitants. These were students from the evacuated Rachel Macmillan Nursery Teachers' Training School at Deptford. In 1943 a German bomber disintegrated over Hildenborough, and various parts fell on the establishment: the fuselage on the greenhouse, and one of its engines into the lake. The crew baled out, one being captured on the tennis court, one in the drive and one apparently lasted long enough to hide under a bed. I knew one of the students concerned, and she told me that the whole episode considerably brightened their rather cloistered existence.

The last 2½ miles (4 kilometres) of the Medway into Tonbridge is undergoing an important operation, to wit the River Medway Flood Relief Scheme. The Medway and the Eden rivers have a long history of flooding, especially the upper Medway with its many tributaries, as we have seen, rushing down from Ashdown Forest and the High Weald. In July 1968 the former river authority, now called Southern Water, carried out a study to consider ways and means of reducing the flood menace in both valleys. This was an ominous portent, for in September there was a disastrous flood when 9 square miles (24 square kilometres) were under water, and a lesser flood followed in February 1974. The worst part to suffer in these floods was the middle Medway flood plain from Tonbridge to Yalding, being low lying, fertile and intensively farmed. Out of much discussion, not always in agreement, it was decided to construct a scheme that will be the largest on-river flood storage in Britain and unique in design.

The idea is to throttle back flood water in the channel behind a barrier, and to release it under control, so that the river level downstream will never rise above "bank-full" condition, and thus prevent dangerous flooding. This is achieved by having within the barrier a control sluice with three radial gates which will operate automatically according to the actual conditions. The barrier is a 1,300-metre-long and 5.7-metre-high embankment with a core of clay supported by gravel shoulders.

Schemes of this nature are rarely built without difficulty, and the problem here has been that the embankment crosses or interferes with many other river features such as the Powder Mill Cut, the river itself, the railway embankment, the Tonbridge by-pass bridge, a gravel plant, Hayesden lagoon, and finally two silt lagoons (old gravel workings). The six-arch railway bridge, for example, has had to have its foundations protected by gabions. These are wire baskets filled with stone—familiar objects throughout Europe along fast-flowing rivers that tend to flood. Here the gabions have been filled with Kentish rag and put along the arches. Leigh village has been protected by a new pumping station, and the grand result of all these works will be that in a flood of the 1968 type, or once in a hundred years, the Medway valley from Penshurst to here would become a vast temporary lake for about three days.

Environmental problems delayed the scheme for about a year, and sadly some of the present river landscape will disappear. The new river channel will mean the end of the old sluice and weir pool that was such a favourite spot for anglers and the head of "navigation" for canoes. I have walked all round the area and talked to the engineers involved, and on balance I think they have done their best in a part of the valley that had great interest to naturalists; and always in the background there is the pressure of the urban fringe, for we are fast approaching our first Medway town—Tonbridge.

6

Plain Mother and Elegant Daughter—
Tonbridge and Tunbridge Wells

From Penshurst the approach by river to Tonbridge has the great advantage of arriving in the old town centre without any of the tedious threading of modern dreary suburbs that afflict so many English towns. Along the green water meadows and among the marshy channels of the river the traveller is given a very pleasant introduction to this Medway waterside town. Its siting was indirectly due to the local geology, for an extremely convenient outcrop of sandstone is on the north side of the river, and the flood plain narrowed enough for early man to take advantage of a rather rare fording point.

The Medway valley on either side of the town floods easily, and this has rather ironically preserved the older interesting core, because the great wave of mid-twentieth century building has been north and south of the old High Street. This has made the present shape of Tonbridge rather like a neatly tied bow where the High Street crosses the river, with the northern "wing" beyond the Public School rather larger than the southern one beyond the railway station.

It is certainly a very old site, but the peopling of it is obscure. Whatever settlement existed was included in the Saxon lathe of Elesfort, the Royal manor of Aylesford. These lathes were ancient divisions of Kent, and Elesfort was a natural unit that followed the Medway valley from Hoo near the mouth right up to the fringe of the forested High Weald above Tonbridge. They have a shadowy origin, and as Elesfort consisted of that part of Kent that had been closely lived in during Roman and British tribal times, these lathes are probably much older than the Saxon and Jutish boundaries.

Tonbridge's name, which seems so straightforward, has an equally confusing origin; by Domesday it was Tonebricg, but whether this meant "town of bridges" over the Medway's former many channels or a personal name, "Tunna's bridge", is not clear. It might even be from the earlier Celtic "dun burgh" or "burig" meaning hill fort, and this could refer to the rather mysterious Iron Age hill fort at Castle Hill 1¾ miles (3 kilometres) away and 400 feet (125 metres) up in the High Weald off the Hastings road (A21). This seems to have been a defensive outpost watching over what even then was a vital fording point across the marshy Medway in a gap of the great enshrouding oak forest of the Kentish Weald.

Whatever its obscure origins may have been, the town is a good example of a place that has throughout the centuries been influenced by its communications. The history of its growth is the history of its transport, whose different elements passed through the cycle of birth, growth to a zenith, decline, disuse and sometimes rebirth.

The river Medway is the oldest of these elements and in those shadowy prehistoric times hindered man's movements until the isolated ford was able to be controlled and defended. The Normans, who had a quick eye for such things, soon grasped this strategic fact and quickly built a wooden palisaded castle on an earth mound or motte 65 feet (20 metres) above the river, still there and now covered with trees. The wooden castle inevitably got burnt and was replaced by the familiar stone keep, and for half a millennium the castle and river were together part of the town's life. Its early career was bloody and stormy and involved Bishop Odo of Bayeux's abortive revolt against his nephew William Rufus in 1088, and a power struggle which continued for 250 years and included the owners' quarrels with Thomas à Becket; their names are—like Tonbridge's—confusing, for the original builder was known by his various fiefs, but the family name that has come down is de Clare.

The fine gateway and inner bailey which you can see now on the river banks were built about 1220–40, and then the castle appeared as a true fortress with four great round towers. There were three sets of machiolations for dropping nasty things on besiegers, a drawbridge and a portcullis. This didn't seem to satisfy Richard de Clare, the castle's lord, so he got Henry III's permission (not very easy) to dig a ditch round the medieval town under the present High Street, along the north edge now called Bordyke, and down to the river again below the bridge. Tonbridge was now virtually an island defended by water. The ditch has long gone, but there is a fragment inside the churchyard wall of the twelfth-century parish church in Bordyke (Borough Ditch) itself.

The castle's influence waned, though it was lived in until 1521 when it became Royal property. In 1646 during the Civil War it was "slighted", that is: unroofed, by Parliament, which started its general decay, helped no doubt by an earthquake tremor which shook the town in 1692. Still, it was not so ruined that

Horace Walpole, visiting Tonbridge in 1751 when a Mr Hooker owned the castle, was "surprised" at its condition; this same owner decided to build a mansion for himself against the gate-house—the stone being as usual filched, this time from the castle itself—in 1793. After this there were many tenants and today only the gatehouse, river-wall and the curtain wall up the mound remain. The local council bought it for offices in 1897 and now it is a sub office of the District Council—an anticlimax to its history which one feels the noble building doesn't deserve.

The river, now freed from its defensive role, had in the mean-time become obstructed with fish weirs—particularly for eels—and water mills. These vested interests of the landowners and farmers who insisted that the river was their private property stopped any other use for centuries, in spite of the Commission-ers for Sewers ordering the removal of the weirs in 1600. In that century the ironfounders' and timber growers' dispute with the farmers and landowners grew—the Weald was the main source of English timber—but it was 1740 before the river was at last made navigable from Maidstone to Tonbridge. Then a Golden Age of river traffic began with bulky and heavy goods like stone and coal coming inwards and timber with Wealden iron going downstream. We know that this iron came from as far away as Heathfield in Sussex, for in 1748 the ironmaster John Fuller sent 289 tons of guns to Woolwich from Brandbridges Wharf at East Peckham to be trans-shipped at Maidstone.

The arrival of stone caused a building boom and two of the town's best inns, the "Rose and Crown" in the High Street and the "Bull" in Bordyke, were refaced as we see them now, and in 1775 the old, almost ruined medieval bridge was rebuilt.

As trade got bigger so did river craft—many were up to 40 tons burden—but their journey up river was a pretty painful affair for it was a manhandling labour until a towpath for horses was made. The zenith of all this effort was perhaps reached by about 1824 when William Cobbett saw Tonbridge and remarked: "Tonbridge is a small, but nice town with some fine meadows and a navigable river."

However, setbacks were ahead, for in 1828 the navigation company became involved in a Chancery suit with the rival Penshurst Canal Company and lost heavily financially, one result being that the ancient channels of the Medway were reduced to two—the present river and the Botany stream. They managed to keep going by supplying the new gasworks with coal by river in 1836, but the long slow decline started in earnest when six years later the railway arrived. The Company made the historical error of trying to compete instead of co-operating as they refused to supply coke to the railway (early locomotives burned coke) and afterwards throughout the century managed their affairs badly. The river was becoming dirty too at Tonbridge; the town was insanitary with zymotic diseases—among them cholera—and the 1854 death rate was above average, and half of those who died were under fifteen.

Trade continued, but the lucrative hop traffic went in 1891, gasworks coal in 1902 and at length in 1911 the company was wound up, and the Upper Medway Conservancy Board assumed public control. They closed the river for four years whilst ten new locks were built, flood control improved and efforts were made to maintain navigation; but the public purse was not bottomless and in 1934 commercial navigation ceased—and after nearly 200 years the river resumed its placid timeless way. Two post-war efforts tried to revive it with the Gas Board's experiment in towing a 200-ton barge to Tonbridge in 1950, and two years later the 82½-ton lighter *Medrobin* made a remarkable but slow voyage from Maidstone. Her 80-foot (25-metre) length found the bends painful, and the three-day voyage took twice the time of the old horse boats—so the cause of river navigation was hardly improved.

The sad truth is that apart from slowness and inconvenience —two things the modern world won't tolerate—much larger and modern locks are needed which would mean canalizing the river and might well spoil the valley; so now the middle course is left for pleasure craft. This means that at times the river is crowded and uncomfortable, as all places are when too many people are all trying to do the same thing. However, at the Town Lock you can still get some innocent fun watching the antics of the apprentice navigators, and have some pleasure in helping with their lines, especially when an old canal longboat is trying to come alongside. The lock gates are now unmanned, so giving a hand with the heavy winch gains surprised but grateful thanks all round. And the river near the bridge has been smartened up by the fine new building of Maylens Wharf.

After the river, the road forms the second element of transport history in the town. The earliest ancestor was the prehistoric ridge way from the North Downs through the Weald crossing the Medway ford at the site of Tonbridge. This linked the Iron Age camps of Oldbury (near Ightham), Castle Hill and Saxonbury at Frant. There is no direct evidence that the Romans used it, but it may have been a minor track for ironworking.

For all that, one of its descendants was the Norman route to the sea from London, and this in turn became the "Rye Road" from Bromley and Sevenoaks through Tonbridge to Rye, and thence to France via Dieppe or Havre de Grace (now Le Havre) and via the Seine to Paris. It was an important route because London's fish supply from the coast, cloth by packhorse, and cattle all passed along it.

But from medieval times onwards it was usually in a terrible state, especially across the Weald Clay, and at times was useless for carts and waggons and not very easy for mounted travellers. The side roads from Tonbridge were so bad as to be virtually non-existent, and in 1600 it took two years for timber from the woods near the town to reach the dockyards at Chatham. Even Celia Fiennes on her horse in 1697 found the road from Tonbridge to Sevenoaks "a sad deep clay way after wet". And in 1751 when Horace Walpole wished, as he put it, to "escape to Penshurst" he found "the only man in the town who had two [horses] would not let us have them because the roads were so bad". Rennie, the canal engineer (father of the great Sir John Rennie), when surveying the Weald from Tonbridge as late as 1803 for the projected Grand Southern Canal from the Medway to Portsmouth, remarked that "The country is almost destitute of practicable roads . . . the interior untraversed except by bands of smugglers . . ."

However, Napoleon came and went and John Macadam appeared, with the roads improving perhaps for the first time since the Romans, and the great, robust and apparently jolly era of coaching commenced, as did the age of steam. In 1835 a firm called Ogle & Summers brought a steam carriage to Tonbridge and kept it at the chief coaching inn, the "Rose and Crown", for a week making local excursions. It bowled along at 25 miles an hour (40 kilometres an hour) and might have had a future, but alas, they were sixty years ahead of their time, for in 1836 the "Red Flag Act" was passed, not to be repealed until 1896.

But coaching for all its glamour was expensive. In 1840 to go 30 miles (50 kilometres) from Tunbridge Wells to St Leonard's on the Sussex Coast cost as much as a fortnight in good lodgings. With the advent of the railway the roads were for sixty years almost empty, local and quiet. Then slowly, painfully and with many noisy bangs came the motor car; the first in Tonbridge was a Benz owned by a local jeweller, Alfred Cornell, who was promptly fined for driving it too fast. And then rather incredibly in 1920 this small town tried to have its own car industry, for the firm of Storey produced, amongst others, a four-seater saloon, the "Tonbridge", priced at £1,200—not surprisingly the firm were bankrupt by 1921.

Up to 1939 the main roads were still reasonably adequate, except at week-ends when they became noisy, smelly and crowded as South London set off for the sea via Sevenoaks and Tonbridge. Since the war the crucial position of the town at the junction of two main roads, the A21 and A26, from London and Maidstone to the south coast, plus the A227 road to Gravesend, has meant a gigantic pile-up of traffic along its old High Street. In 1971 the long-suffering townspeople got their by-pass. But the work was delayed and the cost mounted because boreholes in the Quarry Hill brickworks discovered the true nature of an ancient geological fault. The proposed cutting here and under the Southborough road had to be widened. From the top of the bridge complex near Mabledon Hospital, a house that Decimus Burton built in 1831, there is a fine panorama of Tonbridge in its Medway setting, inexorably spreading across the Low Weald.

The railway, the third transport element, is young and its arrival in Tonbridge in May 1842 was almost accidental; nevertheless it has caused the most change. The South Eastern Railway had come from London by a very roundabout route via the Redhill junction of the Brighton Railway. The company's engineer, famous later as Sir William Cubitt, had decided that the ancient Roman Watling Street route was physically beyond the efforts of those early locomotives, and even the later more direct route proposed to Tonbridge via Oxted was rejected on account of the very heavy engineering works involved. The line continued to Ashford, dead straight and with slight gradients for 26 miles (42 kilometres), reached Folkestone by June 1843 and, with a slight delay, Dover (where part of the Round Down Cliff on the Kent coast was blasted into the sea). The S.E.R. took about three hours for the 92-mile run to Dover, averaging nearly 30 miles (48 kilometres) an hour, whilst the mail coach took three times as long, and was slow, expensive and uncomfortable. So the advantage of the railway was obvious.

The effect on the town was magnetic, the town going to the railway rather than the railway coming to it, for in spite of the station being half a mile away beyond the river it drew settlement quickly. Local geology was again convenient; a patch of dry sandy brickearth made a base for the station yard and engine shed, and provided ballast for the track. So Tonbridge became a railway town, and so in some ways it still is. The town changed its name (from Tunbridge), but the railway retained the old spelling for another fifty years.

This was an exciting period packed with incidents, like Napoleon III's train which stopped before a large welcoming crowd in 1855, and the Sultan of Turkey's train later which was supposed to but didn't! It caught Charles Dickens's imagination too, for in a little sketch written in 1851 called "A Flight" he described a trip to Paris via the S.E.R. "I fly away among the Kentish hops and harvest . . . the Guard appears . . . 'Are you for Tunbridge, sir?' 'Tunbridge? No, Paris.' 'Plenty of time, sir. No hurry. Five minutes here, sir, for refreshment'."

Then, the S.E.R., whose reputation had stood high, was involved in a long cold war over thirty years with its brash rival, the London Chatham & Dover, led by their respective chairmen, Sir Edward Watkin and James Staats Forbes. Watkin, a Cobdenite Liberal, was a stern and ruthless character but also a man of great vision. His schooling in the tough northern railway world had led to his chairmanship of the Manchester, Sheffield & Lincolnshire. He dreamt of a direct Manchester-Paris rail-link using the long straight level Wealden route across Kent and Surrey avoiding London, with a Channel Tunnel as the apex of his achievement. The S.E.R. started the tunnel, but owing to an extraordinary snowballing military scare it was abandoned in 1883, although now it is pretty certain that the wily Forbes turned the War Office against Watkin's scheme. In the meantime it had become a national affair.

Here one can pause to think about the position of Tonbridge if the tunnel had been built, for the town would have been the great exchange junction for London. Would it have spoilt some of its amenities? I doubt it—far less than overcrowded roads and suburban expansion that has followed in the wake of the motor-car age. After years of frustration and political debate, short-sighted insularity and the mounting cost, the chances of one still seem remote, although a single-line bore has recently been proposed which seems to satisfy British and French Railways but not apparently the politicians. Richard Church, who was a great Kentish patriot, wrote some years ago: "For years I waited for news of the making of the Channel Tunnel, and I would look wistfully from the boat train as it slipped into the tunnel through the Shakespeare Cliff, for just at its entrance stood the works where the abortive attempts to start the great undersea junction with France were begun . . ." It is interesting to reflect that the

Japanese are currently building the world's longest undersea railway tunnel between the islands of Honshu and Hokkaido 33 miles (54 kilometres) long, and it is more than half finished!

On a note of nostalgia, Tonbridge was a good place to see the steam-hauled expresses of the old Southern and later Southern Region. The passage of the "Golden Arrow" Pullman boat express with a "Lord Nelson" or later Bulleid Pacific was a great flash of green, gold and chocolate—about the finest train Kent ever saw and the only train to race a homing pigeon which it just won in 1932. The Hastings trains via Tunbridge Wells pulled by the handsome smaller, but powerful, "Schools" class were worth watching too, and there was always something interesting coming from Redhill and distant Reading on the old Wealden Line. After 1868 this route was never quite used to its full potential following the opening of the direct line to London by the long tunnels of Sevenoaks and Polhill, but its strategic advantage plus the Channel Tunnel could make it a line of the future.

But the magnificent steam age of Britain came to an ignominious end, killed by the mirage of cheap oil and inability to maintain the most sympathetic machines that man ever invented.

Electrification reached Tonbridge by 1960, improving the semi-fast and London services, and by 1963 there were 2,300 season ticket holders. Commuting traffic for the railways is uneconomic and difficult for staffing, and it has always seemed to me that this is not usually understood by the public who in this way see the worst side of train travel.

The fourth element of transport, the air, affected Tonbridge in two isolated periods of history. The first was in 1920 when pilots of the new Croydon-Paris Air Service used to follow the long straight Wealden railway track between Redhill and Tonbridge in their converted Handley-Page bombers. Twenty years later the town was really aware of the air; it was astride the Medway which was followed by German bombers, and great air battles were fought high above the town. Tonbridge reminds its visitors of this with a plaque near the bridge at 111 High Street which reads:

Above this roof the Battle of Britain was fought and won, August 8th–October 10th 1940. This plaque is dedicated to the Few.

So Tonbridge, a small town for centuries in spite of being the largest parish in Kent, has always been a meeting point for all

kinds of transport. Its inns, still some of the finest buildings left,
are the best proof of this; some we have already noted, but the
sixteenth-century timbered "Chequers" in the High Street had
just about the most cheerful and efficient barmaid one could
wish for when I was last there. The small fifteenth-century
house in Bordyke that became a pub, the "Ivy House", is worth
seeing and sampling. If you like to use the fifth element of
transport—your legs—there is a small interesting white
weather-boarded pub with a yellow sign called the "Primrose" on
the Hastings road, and not so much further on is a large hostelry
called "Ye Old Vauxhall Inn"—both part of the town's history.

The cattle-market, for so long the weekly meeting point of the
market town's life, is now closed but past evidence is to be found
in East Street with the Portreeve's House. This fine fifteenth-
century timber-framed building with oriel windows was where
the chief collector of tolls and dues lived; stare and screw up your
eyes and you have old Tonbridge.

Wealden iron was worked outside the town—often on large
estates—but it produced an iron foundry and cutlery trade inside the town; as a character in a seventeenth-century book
says: "I was born near unto Tunbridge, where fine knives are
made". The foundry produced the cast-iron 1887 bridge which
replaced the former rebuilt medieval "petty gothic bridge" that
Walpole admired. The iron bridge is more suited to the kitchen
than the drawing-room, but it has served the town well considering what has thundered over it in nearly a century.

However, apart from boat-building (now plastic), one of the
most interesting trades has been cricket, providing both players
and the materials to play the game. For over a century until
1978 cricket balls were made in the three works on the Medway
banks, and others were up in the Quarry Hill area. One was so
close to the river that the craftsmen quilters and seamers could
hang their fishing rods from the window to make supper more
exciting at the day's end.

Traditionally many Kent players came from the school
founded in 1553 by another of London's affluent Lord Mayors,
Sir Andrew Judde of the Skinners' Company who was a Tonbridge man. This original grammar school divided in 1888 producing a local grammar school called Judd in Brook Street and
the Public School, now an impressive Victorian E-shaped building at the north end of the High Street, but there are outliers
in London Road and the hinterland towards Shipbourne Road.
From here came one of the most affable and capable English

cricket captains, and a delightful stroke player to watch—Colin
Cowdrey. Before leaving the school, its connection with the
river must be noted, and one can do no better than quote the
school itself: "The vagaries of the river Medway make rowing in
Eights impossible, but the school competes in Fours at Head of
the River Races and Regattas . . ."

Tonbridge's great cricketing son was Frank Woolley, although
he wasn't often seen in his native town. He played for Kent,
England and later Bearsted and finally coached at King's
School, Canterbury. R. C. Robertson-Glasgow, the cricket
writer, once said of him, "Easy to watch—difficult to bowl to—
impossible to write about." In the mid-1970s the local club
produced Bob Woolmer who became an England all-rounder.

Today although the town now has 35,000 people, trade and
industry are rather prosaic and small-scale, like the hand-made
bricks still being produced at Quarry Hill and an important
printing works, but it is interesting to note that the railway is
still the biggest employer.

We leave Tonbridge and the Medway and climb up Quarry
Hill to the wooded ridge at Bidborough, where there are fine
views over the Weald, and drop down into the valley of the
Barden stream, at Furnace Farm. Here was the site of the
Barden furnace, one of the many producing cannon for the
Browne family, the Royal Stuart gunfounders. They—like the
Vicar of Bray—kept on casting for the state whilst Royal heads
fell and Cromwell's major-generals ruled, and continued till the
Restoration and the Dutch Wars. The sluice is still there, below
the road next door to a restored mill house. Whilst exploring this
I met the farmer's daughter, a real live shepherdess who intrigued me as she had been to New Zealand to learn the wider
aspects of this now rare (but healthy) job. You can reach here by
a rural side road from Tonbridge where at Brook Street Farm
there are two interesting little roofed open frames atop of which
seemed to be oast kilns. But, alas, the last time I looked, a
demolition firm was at work with a board stating, "Making way
for the future". *O tempora, O mores!*

Higher up the Barden valley is the village of Speldhurst with
a fine pub, the "George and Dragon", where a notice outside
states:

The landlord owns a Boston terrier popularly known as the infamous
"Grouse". This is attributable to his aversion to: (a) other dogs (b)
uniforms (c) gum boots (d) keg beer drinkers. *You* have been warned!

Enough said!

From Speldhurst up again on to the ridge is Southborough, once a hamlet and manor, now a long-drawn-out place completely choked with traffic slowly and continuously groaning past this beautiful village green. This was also a cricket-ball making centre, associated chiefly with the old firm of Thomas Twort, whose wooden works were destroyed by a German V2 in 1944. In the Coronation Year (1953) the new Southborough coat of arms included a cricket ball plus two bricks—from the other industry at High Brooms. Now in 1980 both are defunct, and the coat of arms a memory.

And so to Tunbridge Wells, whose many slopes with tributary streams supply the Medway with much water. This is the elegant grown-up daughter born Cinderella-fashion from a collection of huts and tents beside medicinal iron springs which like those at Bath, as Sam Weller said, tasted of "warm flatirons". They had been accidentally discovered in 1606 by the young courtier Lord North whilst riding in the woods south of Tonbridge. He had soldiered in the Low Countries, and had tasted similar waters at Spa in what is now Belgium, the town that gave its name to all such places the world over. They soon attracted attention, but there was nowhere to stay other than the tiny villages of Rusthall and Southborough so Tunbridge became a base for the unbuilt spa. Some of the fashionable gentry from London—ill, old or just worn out—camped al fresco on the surrounding hills, or like Henrietta-Maria, the determined and diminutive Queen of Charles I, were housed in marquees on the Common. She did this in 1629 when taking the waters before the birth of a son, and was so pleased with the result that some wished to christen the new spa, "Queen Mary's Wells". However, considering what was to follow during the Restoration Court period it perhaps was as well they stuck to the name of nearby Tunbridge.

As with most spas at this time, taking the waters was for many a convenient pretext for other diversions, which prompted the French Ambassador to the Court, the Comte de Grammont, to comment, "Well may they be called les Eaux de Scandale, for they have nearly ruined the good name of the Maids and the ladies—those who are there without their husbands."

All this meant that the early growth was untidy with much illicit building of houses, shops and taverns near what is now the Common. Here an interesting parallel existed with Greenwich (then in Kent) where the same thing happened on the edge

of Blackheath; the subsequent history of Blackheath village is
close to that of Tunbridge Wells.

Remarking in 1697 on the buildings of the spa, Celia Fiennes
—the lady traveller who rode side-saddle around England—
apparently after sampling the waters, said that the town included two large coffee houses, two lottery and hazard rooms, a
number of apothecaries' shops and several bowling greens.

Religious action and reaction have left a certain mark in the
town for the Restoration revels annoyed the Dissenters who
named the prominent hills Mount Ephraim, Mount Pleasant
and Mount Sion. This puritanism was met by the dedication of
the church—at first a chapel-at-ease—in 1678 to Charles the
Martyr. Originally this building had its altar in Tonbridge
parish, the pulpit in Speldhurst and the vestry in Frant (Sussex)
parish. The church itself was not completed until 1696. Outside
it is rather plain, but inside it has a fine plaster ceiling with an
octagonal dome supported by two columns. The roof breaks the
plainness by having a white weather-boarded belfry with a clock;
this church has a "twin" in another new town built at the same
time, Falmouth in Cornwall.

Tunbridge Wells in some ways was a pioneer in sanitation
and town planning, as there were special covenants regarding
the height of buildings and sewerage along the parade known as
the Walks which led to the chief drinking well. From this came
the Queen Anne inspired "pedestrian precinct" of the Pantiles,
the chief glory of the old spa town with its fine Tuscan columns
and line of elms; but the original square pantiles have gone,
replaced in 1793 by large flags, which still remain.

The spa period, which soon became a gambling one as well,
reached its peak in the middle Georgian times following the
arrival of Beau Nash from Bath in 1735. This rather scandalous
era has left the fine legacy of some eighteenth-century houses,
like the double-fronted ones with iron balconies in Mount Sion.
The decline of the spa was caused largely by the rise of Brighton,
where in 1730 a certain Dr Russell M.D. had advocated sea-
bathing, so salt water became fashionable instead of unpleasant
fresh water.

The town was for a long time really a group of four villages:
the original spa town, Mount Ephraim, with more permanent
residents above the common with its sandstone tors and trees;
Mount Sion with its lodging houses above the Pantiles; and
(later) Mount Pleasant north of Mount Sion (now a tree-lined
shopping street above the Central Station). The linking of these

areas began with a Scottish builder named James Haliburton who had a tenth son, born in 1800 and named Decimus, who later shortened his surname to Burton. He became an architect, like Nash, and as Nash transformed Bath so Decimus Burton transformed Tunbridge Wells in the late 1820s. He built in Wealden sandstone, the blocks being quarried at Tonbridge (Quarry Hill) and over the years designed an entire planned townscape.

This was in five parts beginning westwards with Church Road, where there is Holy Trinity Church built in 1827 in Gothic style (not his best building), and the Priory in Tudor style (now offices). Then eastwards into Crescent Road; after this on the right Calverley Terrace and Parade with the Calverley Hotel where Queen Victoria stayed before Burton made it into a hotel; then Calverley Road to Camden Road, and finally to Calverley Park. Inside here Calverley Park Crescent forms Burton's most splendid memorial. This is an arc of large houses with a colonnade of Roman arches supporting two Greek pavilions and Doric pilasters, for Burton built mainly in the Greek Revival style—the last to do so, which for Victorian England was a great pity. Among his other buildings are the Athenaeum in London in 1827 and the Regent's Park Colosseum in 1823.

In 1846 the South Eastern Railway arrived by a difficult route with tunnels and the station (now Central) was built in a pleasing Italianate style; this is now on the Up side, as the station was later expanded—which altered the effect. Later the Brighton Company (the L.B.S.C.R.) reached the town at what is now Tunbridge Wells West, being brought round afterwards through a single line tunnel to the Central Station in 1881. The railways touched off a period of elegance and well-ordered civilized urban living encouraged by the young Queen Victoria, and this lasted almost a century. During this long era it was an elegant town set amid the beautifully hilly landscape of the High Weald, which could be visited leisurely by train along branch lines or horse-drawn vehicles of all kinds. Slowness didn't really matter; this was the relaxed graceful living with the Empire at its height, neither ever to be seen again.

The town had also natural attractions in the outcrops of sandstone, reflecting a past climate, such as the High Rocks—once an Iron Age hill fort with earthworks used probably until the Roman period. The curious Toad Rock at Rusthall inspired a small boy to escape from his nursemaid and climb it, afterwards becoming President of the Alpine Club. He was Sir Martin

Conway, later Lord Conway, who restored Allington Castle. Dunorlan Park illustrated the Victorian wider sense of curiosity for exotic trees with its many fine large conifers. But the Imperial decline meant inevitably the decline and change of the town's character.

Since 1960 it has seen a period of uncertainty coupled with urban expansion, much of it out of character and built for social and commercial reasons rather than to blend or harmonize with the existing townscape. The worst features of the car age are present in the choked roads and overcrowded streets of a Wealden town in ridge-and-vale country not suited to heavy road traffic. The rail connections were amputated without enough protest so that you cannot go to either Brighton or Eastbourne by rail, and when belatedly British Rail tried to improve matters with the Hastings electrification due for completion in 1985 and wished to alter Grove Hill tunnel the protests sounded rather false to me. (No one, it seems, minds destroying the countryside for a motorway, but to pull down one house and cause some inconvenience for the sake of a railway is apparently sacrilege!)

However, there is much good cultural activity within the town, and they are still outward-looking in their European connections, especially the link with another elegant spa town in Germany, Wiesbaden. Some later building has definitely restored welcome elegance in the Neo-Georgian development of Trinity Close off the Pembury Road. And I was pleased to see Decimus Burton "reborn" in the good-looking new houses built in his style at Lansdowne Square. Expensive, did I hear you say? Of course. All beautiful buildings always were; I don't suppose the building of classical Athens or Rome was exactly cheap, but what a heritage they have left us.

7

The Middle Medway and down the Shode

Downstream from the Town Lock at Tonbridge the Medway begins its middle course which divides neatly into two contrasting river landscapes. First comes the flood plain across the Low Weald to Twyford near Yalding, and then the valley gap through the Greensand Ridge to Maidstone.

The wide valley from Tonbridge to Twyford has that quality of seclusion which we found from Forest Row to Ashurst, but it is flatter and (surprisingly) more remote. For here is a richly cultivated river lowland devoid of roads and houses except for the isolated traditional Kentish farm buildings like oast kilns, and those that still exist sit well away from the river. The river's course winds through the flat valley with an orchard here and there reaching the water's edge, but for the most part it is a serene landscape of odd alder clumps, groups of willows and isolated oak trees. It is 8 miles (13 kilometres) of splendid waterside scenery at any time of the year and in almost any sort of weather if one follows the towpaths on the left bank to East Lock, and then via Branbridges on the right bank to the Anchor Inn at the Teise confluence.

Just outside Tonbridge, at Cannon Bridge, which now carries the "mini by-pass" and is new since 1968 (for the old one was carried away in the great flood of that year), a lane leads off to Postern Forge. Here is a Wealden cottage, now much extended and rebuilt, that is possibly an original ironworker's cottage, for two were known to exist here in 1622. The present owner, Mr Kirk, a London solicitor, very kindly showed me round this interesting house. Whilst doing restoration work he discovered some blue layered Guilloche work (French carved paintwork) as well as some Jacobean oak panelling. His son, Oliver, in 1977 and then aged nine, not to be outdone found a cannon ball in the garden. This was cast when the demand was high, probably during the period of one of the armament "booms" of the seventeenth century, because Postern was a small forge normally making valuable but mundane implements like pots and pans. Flowing through the garden pond and the remains of a "straight cut" (to straighten the stream for increasing its flow for the forge) is the Waites stream which supplied the power before joining the Medway further north.

Beyond here past Postern itself, a mid-Georgian house with fine gardens, the lane now in open country reaches the great estate of Somerhill. This was carved out of the 5,000-acre (2,000-hectare) forest of Southfrithe between Tonbridge and what is now Tunbridge Wells which was disparked in the sixteenth century. The present Jacobean house was built about 1614 by the Earl of Clanricarde on the site of a house that once belonged to Sir Philip Sidney. Earlier inhabitants are said to have indulged in riotous living, but the Earl's granddaughter, Lady Purbeck, carefully divided some of the Somerhill land as sites for leased lodging houses on a hillside known later as Mount Sion in Tunbridge Wells.

During the nineteenth century the house was restored by the d'Avigdor-Goldsmid family who have been prominent in Tonbridge local affairs, Parliament and the Services. The present owner is Lady d'Avigdor-Goldsmid, and you can walk through much of the grounds around the large lake through which the Waites stream flows to the Postern Forge. They are very spacious and beautiful with two huge old Scotch pines and magnificent Blue Atlas cedars in the gardens behind the house. This whole scene with views over the still extensive relics of Southfrithe Forest on the rising ground of the High Weald out of sight and sound of the eternal traffic noise of the 1980s can take the mind back hundreds of years to an earlier wilder and quieter Wealden landscape.

In a remote corner of these grounds called Devil's Gill Straker discovered the remains of a medieval iron bloomery, of great interest because it is the only Wealden one of which the accounts survive. Its position was certainly strategic, being near the Medway bridge at Tonbridge, protected by its castle, and had for its market the rich plain of the Kentish Low Weald. The forge worked from 1329 to 1361 before being suddenly overwhelmed by the second outbreak of the Black Death, giving us a brief insight into what was a frightening period in our history.

Somerhill is in the parish of Tudeley where the church on an old Saxon site, and now rather rebuilt, has in its east window a beautiful piece of modern stained glass by Marc Chagall. This was a memorial to Sarah, the daughter of Sir Henry and Lady d'Avigdor-Goldsmid tragically lost by drowning. In Provence recently I came across another example of Chagall's work in the Romanesque cathedral of the little town of Vence, where he had made a mosaic on seventeenth-century plaster carvings. On returning to Tudeley I was angry and saddened to discover that the east window had been damaged from the outside by unknown mindless descendants of those fifty-century barbarians. The church was locked, as many now regrettably are, and may well explain the damaged window in the true mode of the Vandal: what we can't steal we shall destroy.

Nearby here is a field which saw a great event in 1931 when the Imperial Airways "Hannibal", one of those curiously asymmetrical but stately old biplanes on the London–Paris service, was forced down with its eighteen passengers, none of whom was injured.

Tudeley is in the hop and fruit belt which spreads eastwards to Paddock Wood and Marden, and northwards to Maidstone with an intense hop area around Yalding to Hunton. Hops were probably first imported by the Flemish weavers at the beginning of the sixteenth century; the word is from the old Dutch or Flemish *hoppe*. Leonard Mascall of Plumpton is said to have introduced them to Sussex in 1525, where they spread to Surrey, and today there is still a small concentration on the light sandy soils around Farnham. Kent, it seems, received the hop in 1550 when the first French Huguenot refugees landed at Sandwich by invitation of Edward VI, but they may have brought the method of cultivation rather than the plant itself. The improved method of roasting them came from Flanders about 1584. And from all this, beer became an English drink, supplanting ale.

Cultivation was slow at first owing to high costs to pay for such things as manure for fertilizing (it is a greedy feeder), hop poles (competition from clothiers and ironworkers), picking and drying, and often total loss from bad weather. As this period was the so-called "Little Ice Age" following the dry and warm medieval period, the summers were wet and cool and winters cold and frosty. Professor Lamb, the meteorologist, thinks the hop pole may originate from the early English vineyards where vines were trained on high poles. Once the hop did spread the profits were high with fairly easy transport to the local brewers, and supplying the huge London market via Rochester or along the Medway from Tonbridge.

There is no doubt there was overproduction in the past reaching its peak in the 1920s, which led to price cutting and chaotic marketing. The Hop Marketing Board was formed in 1932 to arrange quotas for what was then a domestic and captive market. However, since the last war the world of beer-drinking has changed and the public has preferred less "bittery" beers, so there has been a rise in lager beer drinking, not realized at first by brewers and growers.

There are many varieties of hops, but broadly they are in two classes: High Alpha and Aroma. The first makes beer bitter and the second gives flavour and aroma. It is sometimes forgotten that there is a large world market and world production of hops outside Britain, particularly in the U.S.A., and it is a very valuable export. This was realized in 1972 when, on the eve of entry into the E.E.C. and a free market, one famous brewer said hop growing had suffered from the narrow conservatism of the brewers and unenterprising attitude of growers represented by the Hop Marketing Board. The trend was in High Alpha seedless hops, and if the English hop industry was to be a force in world markets and not the odd man out everyone must cooperate. All this was in sharp contrast to the high technical standards of the hop varieties produced by the research stations at East Malling, Wye College and Rosemaund. Since then the Hop Marketing Board has changed its ideas and the organization is much more liberal. Many more seedless hops are grown, with new varieties being planted every three to four years, developed to a high standard at Wye College. There is now a surplus for export, and English hops are now very good, some going for example to Belgium for the brewing of special traditional beers produced in small breweries there.

Hops led to an interesting architectural development, for (until recently) the oast kiln has provided Kent and Sussex with a distinctive and attractive building. These familiar circular oasts date only from 1835 when they were first designed by John Read and subsequently built in Kentish ragstone, flint or brick, depending where they were. They had special tapered tiles and picturesque white-painted ventilator cowls with their wind vanes. The new design was so popular that all the original buildings have disappeared; later came a pyramid form which was easier to roof with the mass-produced flat tiles and slates, but both are now obsolete, and thus has passed another era of traditional building of no great age.

In 1971 I visited Sherenden Farm in Tudeley to see the latest method of hop drying with thermostatically controlled oil-fired ovens. The foreman admitted that they were a great deal more efficient than the older coal-fired oast kilns, which he said were, "very erratic. But," he added, "they made better beer."

At length we come to Paddock Wood where the Hop Marketing Board has its home in this rather unattractive township, which grew as a railway junction settlement and now, through unfortunate planning legislation, has a most unsuitable heavy truck terminal. The site, however, is very old for it was where the Saxon swinemote was held to discuss all matters of pannage and enclosure. The pigs originally roamed at will through the dense Wealden woodlands and it was the job of the swineherd to keep track of them. Later the pigs were pastured in clearings or "dens" and from these came human settlements; as we have seen, there are nearly 500 "dens" in Kent alone.

However, the railway history of the town is interesting for many reasons, and the station was important from the outset as along with Tonbridge it was where the South Eastern used to "slip" coaches, a curiously British practice which the old Great Western kept up for many years on the Cornish Riviera Express, but the S.E.R. ceased in Victorian times. This system meant that an express could take its passengers for inter-mediate towns en route, without itself stopping, by detaching separate coaches controlled by a guard who then brought them into the station. Its other advantage was reducing the weight of a train before sharp adverse gradients as the G.W.R. did in the hilly south-west of England.

The original station was called "Maidstone Road", built in 1844, and a branch followed the Medway valley via Maidstone to Strood; this is thankfully still with us, electrified, and pro-vides a very pleasant way of seeing the river. In 1848 Charles Dickens wrote to his biographer, Forster, thus: "You will come down booked for Maidstone (I will meet you at Paddock Wood) and we will go thither in company over a most beautiful little line of railroad."

Dickensian fans will remember in *Dombey and Son* Carker's wild flight from Dijon, when he had been spurned by Edith Dombey, which resulted in his death by train at a railway junction after recognition by Mr Dombey. There seems little doubt that this was Paddock Wood, for Dickens knew it very well.

A modern author, C. Northcote Parkinson, has written a masterpiece of historical fiction woven so close to actuality that only a sound knowledge of Napoleonic and Early Victorian events would betray its fictional background. This was the *Life and Times of Horatio Hornblower*, published in 1970 and con-ceived from the late C. S. Forester's immortal character in the old British Navy of wooden walls. It is—as with Dickens in real life—1848, the crisis year, and Prince Louis Napoleon Bonaparte (later Emperor Napoleon III) has been exiled in London; he is suddenly in a great hurry to get to Paris via Dover. In error he leaves the train at Paddock Wood to join the Maidstone branch train which later in torrential rain finds the line blocked at Nettlestead, near the Medway. Prince Louis contemplates returning, but a landslide blocks the route back to Paddock Wood. Somehow he finds Smallbridge Manor, nearby, where Admiral Lord Hornblower lives in retirement and who of course helps the Prince on his way to Paris, ably assisted by Lady Hornblower, and where he wins the Presidential election. We shall refer to this book later with its ingeniously contrived historical geography of the Medway valley.

There was another branch from Paddock Wood, which never paid and "Emmett-like" wound through the hop-gardens to Horsmonden and at a distance surveyed the hilltop town of Goudhurst before rambling on to Hawkhurst. I travelled on it once and found it quite exciting with its deep cuttings and long tunnel. The traffic of course was sporadic but annually it carried over a million pot plants for the hopping traffic; now it is but a nostalgic memory.

Paddock Wood station was the great entrepôt for the hopping traffic and the hop-pickers' trains in the days when the Cockneys left their little terrace houses in the smoky metropolis in great hordes for the Kentish fields. The trains were often dirty, uncomfortable and ill-lit, but they would have delighted the steam vintage enthusiasts for they were often headed by many of the older S.E. and L.C.D.R. engines of the Stirling and Kirtley eras which hauled an incredible variety of elderly carriages and later the famous "Bird Cage" sets of the South Eastern & Chatham Railway.

South of Tudeley by way of country lanes with such whimsical names as Bouncer's Bank and increasingly wooded slopes as one pushes higher into the Weald lies Hawkwell House, associated with Robert Browning. Here in most beautiful grounds with some fine exotic trees and new modern buildings is Kent College Girls' School of Methodist foundation whose reputation has grown in recent years. Hard by is the ancient Pembury parish church, whose village, like so many, moved to another site on account of plague and pestilence.

But we must return to the river. After it has flowed through Eldridges Lock and then Porter's Weir and Sluice it reaches Hartlake Bridge which carries one of the few roads in the flood plain section across the river from Tudeley to Golden Green.

This is a rather plain concrete structure with unusually high parapets which recall a tragic accident. This was on 20th October 1853 when thirty-two hop-pickers were killed because the cart in which they were returning from the hop-gardens at Thompson's Farm, Golden Green, crashed against the rotten parapet of the old wooden bridge and was hurled into the Medway. For some years afterwards a wreath of hops used to be thrown into the river on the anniversary. One of the girl pickers had the rather strange name of Mary Quarium.

Beyond Hartlake the orchards come closer to the river, and in the distance can be seen a new but beautiful sight in Kentish fields during the month of May. These are the crops of oilseed rape, a useful break crop for farmers, a source of oil for soft margarine, honey for bees and a mass of bright yellow flowers for the traveller to behold. Readers of Guy de Maupassant's marvellous short stories written about a century ago, which often concern the peasant of his native Normandy, may recall that colza (an alternative name from the French *kolza*) crops figure prominently; the oil was used for lamps—and it still is in many British lifeboats.

Then comes East Lock, a typical standard Medway type originally built in 1914 by the old Upper Medway Conservancy Board, the public body that tried to keep the navigation alive and were later succeeded by the Kent River Board who built a new steel sluice gate in 1958. Each time I see this lock I am reminded of flooding, for it was this middle valley that took the full force of the September 1968 floods. In February 1974 water again covered the fields and I remember having to climb a tree in order to drop down on to a less deep part of the submerged towpath near East Lock.

Beyond are Oak Weir Lock and Sluices with Stilstead Farm bridge built in 1957 which leads to the great Whitbread Hop Farm curiously fragmented across three roads, two rivers and a railway line which we shall come to later as its main entrance is at Beltring to the east.

The river bank here is open and pleasant with patches of woodland, and rounding the reach brings us to a footbridge leading to the hamlet of Snoll Hatch and the confluence of the river Shode, or Bourne, on the left bank. This appears to be a placid enough little river, but like the Medway it can flood fiercely; not for nothing is it known locally as the "Buster".

The valley region of the Shode contains several buildings of great interest, and some old houses that are unique in Kent. The

river Shode rises near the Pilgrim's Way on the scarp face of the
North Downs. The origin of this ancient prehistoric trackway
has aroused much speculation; it is at least as old as the Iron
Age, and was later much used by medieval pilgrims to Canterbury because it was a dry-shod path on the chalk throughout the
year. Southwards the stream flows over the narrow fertile belt
of Gault Clay in the Vale of Holmesdale, which was believed to
have been blocked in the Ice Ages by glacial material which
allowed this little Medway tributary to cut back, invade and
capture the headwaters of the Darenth. The river now flows
through country dominated by the new motorway complex of
the M25 and M26, which effectively provides a necessary ring
route south of London. The ransom for this convenience is the
destruction of rural tranquillity, impossible to regain. Nearby is
the much altered sixteenth-century Ightham Court, a large
building and once the home of William James, the friend of Sir
Roger Twysden, a Kentish country gentleman of great spirit
whom we shall hear about later.

Under the Maidstone railway line now goes the Shode and for
a little river it has cut a really spectacular gorge in the limestone of the Hythe beds of the Lower Greensand Ridge. Unfortunately it is an area quite ruined by local quarries, and it is
almost impossible to get near the stream at all. However, it was
here at the one-time Pink's Quarry that an Ightham grocer
called Benjamin Harrison, a fine amateur naturalist and geolo-
gist, achieved eternal fame in 1891 by discovering fissures full
of an extraordinary collection of Pleistocene, or Ice Age, fossils.
The fossils of musk ox, reindeer, woolly rhinoceros, giant hare,
cave hyaena and eagles, along with flint flakes from early man,
were mainly of the same age and indicated a more severe
climate than now.

Ightham itself is a main road village on the A227 Gravesend
road; the name is a personal one: Ehta's settlement. It has been
saved from extinction by the perilously near A25 by-pass, and
has some very fine timbered houses near the curve of the road.
One that was built in 1555 seems a bit too near, but has apparently survived 435 years of pack-horses, carts, bicycles, steam-
rollers, buses, motor-cars and lorries. It all looked delightful
when I saw it on a sunny May morning; the road was empty, the
commuters absent and the locals were in the pub—a rare peace
hung over the old village houses.

Not far away is Oldbury Hill, a 620 feet high (195 metres),
part of the Greensand Ridge and made of various sandstones

giving a barren soil, wooded and heathy, and sloping away steeply. This is a fine wild area and it is not surprising to find it was once an Iron Age camp with earthworks that run for nearly 2 miles (3 kilometres). The Romans may well have used it for ironworking, and the later Saxons recognized what it was for the name means "old-fort"; it is the finest hill fort in the Medway region. On the east side are the famous Lower Palaeolithic (Old Stone Age) rock shelters: weathered-out hollows in the soft sandrock below the harder stone, and believed to have been used by hunters incredibly far back in the mists of prehistoric time—perhaps over 100,000 years ago.

Beyond its gorge the Shode flows to Basted, where there were once paper mills that made postage stamps, but they were flooded in 1968, and since then the site houses a large publishing firm called Butterworths employing many hundreds of people. The grounds are tastefully landscaped with the river flowing through it in a fine cascade. Downstream from here the Shode is in a large gap to Plaxtol, where quite close to the river, but not easy to find, up some lanes, is a pleasant eighteenth-century brick farmhouse called Old Soar. But this is not what we have come to see, for standing next door is an ancient building of Kentish rag, built as far back as 1290. This is part of a medieval manor which, for its size, gives a visitor more idea of the everyday life of the lord and his retainers than any other building that I know of in the Medway region. In those times the hall was the centrepiece of any manor house, where everybody ate and all except the lord and his family slept. They were above in a chamber called a solar, which was also a sitting-room. Off from here was a chapel which doubled as an office and study and a garderobe—or privy. All these were at one end of the hall below which space was used for the storage of the lord's possessions and winter food—very important in medieval times.

The hall itself served also as a manorial courtroom. Here at Old Soar the building is a three-room solar block above a barrel-vaulted storeroom, the hall having been built into the house next door in 1740. However, this is private, but one can stand in the doorway, look and imagine, especially as the manor is believed to have belonged to the Aylesford branch of the ubiquitous Culpeper; here it was William, who died in 1326. They were reputed to kidnap and forcibly marry heiresses, and this made them the largest landowners in Kent and Sussex.

Plaxtol is a hill village with the church at the top, the only complete Kentish seventeenth-century example, being built in

1649 during the Commonwealth period by Archbishop Laud, and hence has no dedication to any Christian saint. It is a Gothic building and surrounded by a vast churchyard in which a great variety of trees flourish, including a large ash and two big Chile pines, and unexpectedly a cremation area.

Not far away are two pubs, the "Papermaker's Arms" and the "Rorty Crankle"; the name of the latter apparently means a corner, or ingle nook, and inside are translations into many different languages. At the bottom of the hill is Hyders Art Metal works, an interesting firm which started as a village industry from carpenters and a forge. It developed steadily over the years into art ironwork with exhibitions of their craft and flourished mightily. The managing director showed me over their showrooms in a marvellous old timber house built in 1395, with superb examples of their craft as well as older work. Unfortunately, this fine ironworking is threatened by very high costs and rather unnecessary trade union activity.

Around Plaxtol amid the woods and orchards, some of which are cultivated nut trees of the Kentish cob or hazel, was found in 1857 a beautiful bronze statuette of Minerva, the Roman goddess, exciting Richard Church, "so that for a second the past comes really to life . . ." For me it means almost the confirmation of Roman life in this area, a thought that crossed our minds at Oldbury.

From Plaxtol it is but a step to Fairlawne, once the home of Sir Henry Vane, executed in 1662 for his Puritanical and Parliamentary beliefs—a rare example of revenge by the Royalists. The house in recent years belonged to the late Major Cazalet of Huguenot descent, of Royal racing fame, but since his death the house has been involved in some extraordinary property deals. The present owners, a development company, are making strenuous efforts, however, to refurbish the estate which contains some fine lakes and exotic trees. Among these are some examples of the large Monterey pine (*Pinus radiata*), a native of a very small area in California, and a tree which shows extraordinary vigour and very odd growth. I have seen huge specimens in New Zealand, far larger than in their native land; some grew 200 feet (60 metres) in forty years. They will grow throughout the year in the far south-west of England, but otherwise they are erratic.

Beyond Plaxtol the Shode passes Roughway paper mills, which still make fine writing paper, and is joined by a stream from Ightham Mote, which like Old Soar is hard to find. Indeed, its seclusion saved this incomparable building from destruction, for it was said that Cromwell's soldiers, bent on destroying it as a Royalist stronghold, got lost in the surrounding Wealden woods. It was lived in by various families, but one—the Selbys—held it for 300 years, and in 1872 it was restored by the architect Norman Shaw. But it was a difficult building to maintain, and it was saved a second time in 1889 when Sir Thomas Colyer-Fergusson bought it as an Oxford undergraduate, and his family literally saved the house from falling to pieces. By 1953 they themselves could no longer afford to maintain it or find any buyer who could live in it. So it was saved a third time by an American, Mr Robinson, who for thirty years had cherished a wish to own it, and who has since done all that human endeavour can do to restore it to the world as a perfect example of an early English moated fortified manor-house.

The "mote" of course meant "moot" or meeting-place of Saxon origin, showing that the site itself is older than the buildings of Sir Thomas Cawne in 1340. It is a complex building, but beautifully compact from its first fourteenth-century square of buildings completed down the ages to the second quadrangle outside of Elizabethan construction for staff and stables, some of which survives. Inside you can see that it has been continuously lived in: sixteenth-century Dutch stained glass in the fine chapel; Jacobean staircases; late seventeenth-century Venetian wallpaper; Victorian bedrooms; and twentieth-century oak decoration. And outside there is an eighteenth-century garden. But no more description, go and find it for yourselves (although be warned: it is not often open).

Northwards from here at the hamlet of Ivy Hatch is a house called "Ashwell", and within its grounds is Ightham Vineyard. The owner, Mr Corfe, is a kindly, frank, patient, philosophical person who I think has undertaken the job of English vigneron in the right spirit. The site is sheltered, well drained, sunny and on Greensand loam; the grapes are Reichensteiner, with which he has been experimenting for some years. He has had success with his white wine which has been good enough to be marketed in select hotels. In 1979 his wine was given an English Vineyards Association award for quality. However, in 1980 his crop failed due to the miserable summer, still I could not help thinking that this site was possibly one the Romans may well have chosen in the second century A.D., but their weather was much sunnier and warmer than ours is now.

A mile or so westwards of the Ightham Mote confluence with

the Shode is the large ragstone house of Oxon Hoath, mainly Georgian although some parts go back to the fourteenth century and some forward to the nineteenth, being added by Anthony Salvin of Worth Abbey fame. It was associated with Old Soar and the inevitable Culpeper, Sir John, the grandfather of the unfortunate wife No 5 of Henry VIII, Catherine Howard. The grounds and gardens are the real interest here, particularly the trees with a cedar avenue and some fine oaks behind the house and a view across the large lake to the 170-foot (72-metre) tower of Hadlow Folly sticking up like a lighthouse in the Low Weald. One late December day some time ago I saw the house framed by a rather fine herd of Aberdeen Angus cattle which somehow gave it the right image of the "big house" and broad acres.

Southwards the river is soon on to the flat claylands of the Low Weald, but here over the usual sticky clay is spread that slightly mysterious fine loamy material called brickearth, which the Medway deposited during the melt-water epoch of the Ice Ages. This buff-coloured inheritance from past Arctic climates, along with river alluvium, is the key to the great fertility of the Medway valley from Tonbridge through Hadlow, East Peckham, Yalding and southwards to Paddock Wood. Significantly here at Hadlow is the County Agricultural College whose buildings, cultivated land and experimental orchards are dotted fore and aft of the village.

Hadlow is on the main A26 road to Maidstone with some nice old weather-boarded and tile-hung houses, one being a bakery that produces that rarity in England today—really good bread. The village's other claim to Kentish fame is the extraordinary octagonal Gothic tower built to set off a vast mansion started by Mr Barton May and completed by his son, who also built the tower in the 1830s. The mansion has since gone, pulled down in 1951 except for an enormous ivy-encrusted gatehouse, but the tower is to be preserved.

Hadlow church is the usual interesting assortment of architectural styles, like so many in Kent, with a carved chair inside, which although beautiful seems to be controversial as to its age, and thought at one time to have been used by Miles Coverdale, the sixteenth-century translator of the Bible. The church sits in a delightful little backwater street, which really is the best part of the village.

Onwards from here the Shode flows in two channels to Golden Green, which belies its name as it is rather plain, but sited in very pleasant farmland. I lived here for some years in a rebuilt eighteenth-century brewery cottage with hung tiles, a pretty and pleasant building but whose back garden had been a hop-field. My wife and I had quite a time with it, for generations of cinder and ash had been thrown out by previous cottagers, and the soil beneath seemed drained of its fertility by the former hop plants, for (as we have seen) they are voracious users of the soil.

Where we lived was really Barnes Street, and a few yards down the road are two very interesting buildings, but of quite different history. The first one you come to is a small industrial establishment with quite a history for such a rural area. About a century ago it began life as the Mid-Kent Jam Factory and had a light railway down to the quayside of the Medway. Here coal was off-loaded from the Navigation barges and as a return cargo jam was taken away—some 6,000 tons annually. However, as we have seen, the Upper Medway Navigation either mis-managed its affairs or engaged in uneconomic commerce, and the jam factory soon became bankrupt.

Next came a plastics pioneer, the Crystalate Company, which made early gramophone records (the parent company was in Tonbridge) and billiard balls. The manager was a Mr George Davis who lived in the adjacent house called "The Pines" with a special room that had a high glass dome where his two nephews, Joe and Fred, future world billiard and snooker champions, used to come and try out the balls at the weekends. The firm (as part of a group) is still there, but these days makes rather dull utilitarian plastic pressings.

Walk down the road a few steps and you will see a typical gem of old Kent; what other county has so many beautifully pre-served modest houses? And the Medway valley has its fair share. The gem is the fourteenth-century manor of Barnes Place, actually a sub-manor of Hadlow, held by Tonbridge Castle. The house has a long history with many owners, some of them rather remarkable characters, starting with Richard of Bernes hanged for felony in 1306, when the Crown sequestered the estate. Their interest in the river Medway was important as in 1461 John de Tatlyngbery (a hamlet near Capel) left it to his daughter Alice thus: "his messuage Berne Place water called Okwater [now Hammer Dyke] and weirs, repair of bridge at Hartlake, repair of road between Berne Place and Goldhill and Goldhill and Stair." Today Goldhill House is a farm surrounded by hop-gardens on the Tudeley road over the river, and Stair is a stream that enters the Medway near Tonbridge, and now has no road to it.

Barnes Place had a Tudor tenant for thirty-nine years, Robert White, a tallow chandler, who set up a charity; tallow chandlers were nearly always rich and important for of course they made candles, an essential item in the house. It was sequestered by Parliament during the Civil War, for Hadlow was strongly Parliamentarian, and in 1686 was sold to a Dutch merchant, John Vanhatten. His son was knighted and sold it to Lady Falkland in 1775 whose steward, a Sevenoaks lawyer, lived in it. Gradually it became more connected with farming—as it is today.

The present owner, a resolute lady, has not modernized it, in spite of her doctor's despair at the draughts. She seems healthy enough and is happier than living in a centrally heated red-brick horror. Beauty may be sometimes preferable to comfort, especially when your house has such a history, for in Saxon times the lane by the house led to common water meadows, and these were thought to be on the site of a Bronze Age settlement nearly 4,000 years ago.

From Golden Green the Shode, now a fair stream, flows across the fields between high banks to Little Mill. Along here one fine early March day I saw the local beagle pack cross the river with great gusto in pursuit of a hare, a true countryman's pastime if you don't mind rough cross-country walking. North of here at Kent House Farm six splendid oast kilns have been tastefully and elegantly converted into a fine dwelling. Expensive? Yes, but far better than mouldering into a forgotten ruin.

At Little Mill on the East Peckham road is a fine pub, the "Man of Kent", with the lowest timber beams I have ever found; but in spite of banged heads it is well used and serves good food and drink in a cheerful atmosphere. Opposite is another little industrial site that developed from an old tannery that came from East London, and now makes plastic products. Now called the Brymor Company, it makes very attractive vinyl wall coverings and industrial fire-resistant wallpaper. The Shode water is still used for the boilers that process the paper, and the original tanning process is still used in preparing hides for artificial limbs.

And so to the Medway into which the Shode pours its waters just upstream from the old Branbridges weir and sluice for the mill stream. There was a mill here for many years; this section of the river has a fall of nearly four foot per mile (0.76 metres per kilometre), and at one time (1380) there were eight weirs along it 6–8 feet high (2–2½ metres) which often caused flooding.

After the river was made navigable the mill became involved in a legal actiòn with the Medway Company who lost out financially very heavily indeed in 1751. Their revenge came in a strange way, for a millhand, Henry Boorman (a famous Kentish name), married the millowner's daughter and at length became the mill boss. His nephew rose in the business world, acquired shares and became a director of the Navigation Company, and for a long time the Boormans controlled the river from Branbridges instead of Tonbridge. The mill lasted quite a long time, still grinding flour until the end of the last war, and continued to generate electricity for some years afterwards. Branbridges itself, always an important crossing point, was rebuilt in 1906; it is almost a causeway here, indicating the frequency of flooding.

Nearby is another industrial outlier, although rather untidy in aspect. The original firm here (Arnold & Brandbridges) built a pioneer motor-car in 1896: "The Sociable, a horseless carriage". The present firm (Arnold & Nathan) now produce waste-disposal units, prosaic but necessary adjuncts to our "throw-away" era.

All this district is in the parish of East Peckham, once a pleasant village, a haunt of artists in mid-twentieth century, but now a nondescript, strung-out rural suburb.

South of Branbridges at Beltring is Whitbreads' hop farm, the only one owned by a brewery. Ownership goes back to 1919 when it belonged to E. A. White, a hop-growing expert who produced a good hop called White's Golding on rather poor land—for much of this 1100-acre farm is on Weald clay. Whitbreads bought the farm to ensure continuity of flavour for their bitter beers. I was shown over the farm by the kindness of Mr Pelley, the farm manager, using a Land Rover to traverse main roads and river bridges over the Medway and Shode, not to mention the Maidstone–Paddock Wood railway line. With the brewing changes in recent years the actual hop acreage of different varieties is about 180–200 acres; the rest of the farm is under barley, wheat and pasture. The centrepiece of the farm are the two dozen or so very attractive modern oast kilns near the B2015 road at Beltring, probably the largest group in Britain.

After Branbridges the river flows under the railway line and passes a delightful vista of wooded watery inlets near the grounds of Hale Place. A quiet spot for fishing, where I had an interesting conversation across the river with an old angler who, whilst lamenting the polluted state of the Medway, admitted there were still plenty of "good 'uns" to be caught. The river still has plenty of fish in it, mainly large bream (up to 5 pounds), and reasonable chub and dace; two other species not so well known are carp and the rather small gudgeon. Of course there is also the ferocious and despised pike, but it is perfectly edible, like the pike out of the river Loire in France made into the famous *quenelles de brochet*. But there are English recipes also (Mrs Beeton used bacon), and after all if you don't fancy it, no doubt the cat will if he usually has a tin-fed diet.

On the same bank is the beautifully sited Parsonage Farm-house with surrounding trees and orchards, and at length you approach the outskirts of Yalding. Here at the Anchor Sluices are two steel radial gates which open and close automatically maintaining a constant level upstream. There is also a short weir and the beginning of the navigation "cut-off" via Hamp-stead Lock which avoids the river bend at Yalding. On the left bank near the weir is an old pub, the Anchor Inn, once owned by the Medway Navigation. But in 1871 the company, in desperate financial straits, sold it for £350, and today still with its thatched roof, but much modernized, the waterside area around it in the summer months is a buzzing concourse of activity with pleasure craft, fishermen, spectators and loungers of all kinds.

And just beyond is Twyford Bridge, one of the three old medieval bridges over the middle course; this one is a very solid affair with massive cutwaters, and is rather narrow, and being also long (120 feet, or 37 metres) needed pedestrian recesses— long of course because it spans the Teise as well. We are now at the confluence of what was at one time the most important tributary of the Medway on account of its headwaters being used for ironworking. The bridge has very recently been repaired and modernized with a new terracotta-coloured brick parapet, which I am not sure whether I like, although the work has been executed well enough; I suppose Kentish rag would have been exorbitant—if one could find a mason to do it.

Twyford was the road and river entrepôt for the Wealden ironmasters who shipped their products to Maidstone and thence to London. That is, when they could get them there along the dreadful roads, which were so bad that rates had to be levied in 1584 and 1672 to repair them. The carriers of iron were ordered to make every seventh load one of material to do the repairs with (between October and May). Even then their troubles weren't over for it wasn't until 1580 that even small craft could get upstream to Yalding from Maidstone on account of the obstructions.

8

The Teise and the Beult

The river Teise rises in Chase Wood, part of Waterdown Forest near the Tunbridge Wells–Frant Road, and thus we are back in the High Weald along the Kent–Sussex border, for the river is the boundary here.

The upper course and its headwaters were fundamental to the Wealden ironworkings because of their good flow of water. This wooded region even now has a substantial rainfall annually of 32½ inches (82 millimetres) and in Tudor times (1560 onwards) it probably had rather more. So there was a long string of ponds along the Upper Teise feeding five forges and a furnace; most of their names have gone, but Furnace and Brown's Wood survive (Browne was the Royal gunfounder).

Gone also is the fabulous Commonwealth mansion of Great Bayhall near a tributary in Pembury parish built on the thirteenth-century manor site that was the original home of the Culpeper family. This mansion became the seat of the Camden family and rather strangely disappeared in mid-Victorian times. All that now remains is a pond on a nondescript farm set in this very pleasant ridge-and-vale landscape.

At Tollslye in Furnace Wood the river enters the grounds of Bayham Abbey, old and new. The reedy silted lake is the site of one of the forges which was sold along with the abbey and grounds by Lord Montague, in 1607, who had received it from Queen Elizabeth. Bayham at length passed to the Camdens, who built a new Bayham Abbey in 1870 in the form of a Tudor-style mansion on the crest of the hill overlooking the Teise valley. This family too has now gone, and the abbey ruins remain as a monument to its much earlier founders, the Premonstratensians from the Abbey of Prémontré near Laon in Northern France. Bayham's name is even older, being a Saxon personal one: Baega's hamm or enclosure near the river. The ruins are among the most impressive in southern England, rivalling even those of Fountains, Jervaulx and Rievaulx in Yorkshire, and follow the tradition of certain early orders, with the abbey being sited in an isolated secluded river valley.

On entering the western end of the great chapel or church on the north side of the cloisters, around which it was all built, the immediate impression is of soaring height with its slender narrow lancet windows and pointed arches. This is emphasized by the narrow high nave and the two pairs of transepts. The abbey's life was short, a mere three centuries, but became very much part of local life for on its suppression in 1525 by Henry VIII, the locals tried to restore it to the monks. The abbey, it is said, became lax with good living; a sin I never can quite understand, but then I am no Puritan!

Downstream from the abbey, about a mile from Lamberhurst, is the site of the most famous and largest of the Wealden iron foundries, the Gloucester Furnace. Connected with the works nearby at Hoathly is a sixteenth-century "cut" or canalization of the river to avoid a bend—no small feat of hydraulic engineering for those times. But before going on, digress northwards from here along Hook Lane, and then eastwards to the grounds of Owl House. Here is a perfectly preserved Kentish yeoman's house set in some very fine gardens, with the owl motif prominently displayed on the gateway and walls.

Back to the Teise and the Gloucester Furnace, which lasted (with many owners) for a long time, from 1548 to 1787, and was famous enough to be described by Emanuel Swedenborg, the great Swedish philosopher and mystic. His work *De Ferro* of 1724 has the only known drawing of a Wealden furnace.

This one made vast quantities of cannon, some of which was smuggled to the coast for the use of French privateers, a trade indulged in also by other smaller ironworks in Sussex and undetected until Lamberhurst was found out and heavily fined.

Their most famous product was the greater part of the 200 tons of railings and gates for St Paul's Cathedral, which cost £11,202 at 6d a pound and was transported along the Medway to the Thames. Some of these railings have since travelled further, being preserved as far apart as Toronto and Lewes. They made firebacks here too; now a connoisseur's item, if genuine, but they can all too easily be reproduced. Richard Church, who was a great believer that Kent and Normandy are an identity, that is these two regions are very similar in landscape, cultivation and shared the heritage of France, once bought a fireback at Caudebec on the river Seine with a phoenix design identical to the one he bought many years later in Kent at Cranbrook. However, the best collection of firebacks that I have seen is in the beautiful iron museum of the Fourneau St Michel, near St Hubert in the High Ardennes forests of southern Belgium.

And now we are at Lamberhurst, a main road village on the A21 Hastings highway, still very much unspoilt in spite of its awful traffic noise, with two old inns: "The Chequers" active since 1412 and the younger "George and Dragon". From beer to wine is but a short step for at the top of the hill in the fifteenth-century Priory Farm overlooking the Teise is a vineyard. Started in 1972 and owned by Mr Kenneth McAlpine, it is thoroughly commercially organized, using German methods, equipment and research from the Geisenheim Institute on the Rhine. The site is unusual, being north-facing, but it is sheltered from the prevailing south-westerlies although shelter can often mean too much shade; here the solution has been ingenious windbreaks on the vine wires. Birds were another problem, for having gorged themselves on Kentish cherries over the years, they found Kentish grapes even better and almost demolished the crop in 1974. A special kind of netting known as Blue Wacker has curbed their activities. This commercial winery with its large capacity and huge bottle-storage space can handle wine made by other vineyards, but recent poor yields have meant the capacities are rather under-used. And the quality of the white wine? Well, I have tasted '76, '77 and '78 vintages which I found were all good, made mainly from the hybrid Müller-Thurgau grape. This wine is rather low in acid, being pleasant and mild, which may well suit the general British taste. All in all, this vineyard is honest and open about its successes and failures.

From Lamberhurst the river flows east to the confluence with the river Bewl along a verdant little reach away from roads and houses. In 1976 the quiet upper valley of the Bewl and its tributary, the Hook stream, were transformed by the creation of the Bewl Bridge Reservoir by Southern Water (Kent River & Water Division) to increase water supplies to north-west Kent. Now, you either enthuse over vast artificial sheets of water like this one (770 acres, or 308 hectares) or you don't. I am afraid I do not, for the whole thing seems out of scale and looks wrong, but one must admit that the landscaping has been efficient and care has been taken with the recreational facilities. And that is just the trouble, for the whole effort has been advertised thus: "London need no longer travel to the Lake District or Scotland to dally at a beautiful lakeside" or "leading centre of water sports and amenity". But why can't it be left to the waterfowl and a few trout fishermen and keep its solitude? I am not even sure the wretched thing was necessary, for recently Mr Tom King, Minister of State, Department of the Environment, has said that 50 per cent of our water is wasted by an inefficient system of accounting and assessment.

Near the former river is Chingley Wood where Straker identified a small furnace belonging to Thomas Darell of Scotney. This is interesting because in 1565–6 it supplied iron "plates" for Sir Henry Sidney's steel works at Robertsbridge Abbey. Steel was a rare and expensive item in Tudor times, and difficult to make. For centuries English steel was inferior to the German product from the Siegerland and Sauerland, and no advance was made until 1740 when a Sheffield clockmaker, Huntsman, produced a suitable crucible to make and forge steel ingots.

However, these local ironworks provided the wealth for what we see next. For the jewel of the river Bewl lies across the main road in delectable surroundings, and this is Scotney Castle with its superb landscaped gardens, an all seasons' delight. Years ago I saw it in the bright, clear hard light of an early January day, and gardens, castle and moat looked so enchanting that imagination saw a vanished past of Grimms' fairy tales.

The moated castle with its single wisteria-strewn machiolated tower was built about 1380 by Roger de Ashburnham of Sussex and is all that survives of a castle that looked like Bodiam. Then in the seventeenth century the Darell family, who had lived in it for centuries, rebuilt it and added a new house to the ruins. A famous Jesuit priest, Father Blount, lived here secretly for seven years, for the Darells were a Catholic family. But the great changes were made by the succeeding Hussey family after the Darells' impoverishment, for in 1837 Edward Hussey, a draughtsman and surveyor, built a Tudor house above the valley, designed by Anthony Salvin whose work we met at Worth and Oxon Hoath. This is a truly local house for the stone was quarried from the hill whose strata contain Lower Tunbridge Wells sandstone. It was said that the Husseys were eighteenth-century people living in the wrong century, and this trait seemed to be present in Edward's grandson Christopher. This scholar, journalist, artist, farmer and squire lived there until his death in 1970, and it is to him that the National Trust owes its regional headquarters, an appropriate place indeed.

After Scotney comes the park and fine brick Georgian house of "Finchcocks", named after an earlier family, which Richard Church thought ought to be lived in by "spinsterish connoisseurs" like Alexander Pope or Horace Walpole!

Soon we are in sight of the hill-top town of Goudhurst, and just past the bridge on the A262 is the confluence with the little river Tee, which rises in Bedgebury Park. The estate is extremely ancient and after the medieval Bedgebury family's demise it passed to the inevitable Culpepers; one of them, Sir Alexander, worked the forge here, casting cannon—later for the Armada. The present quite delightful house (now a girls' school) is an extraordinary mixture of a seventeenth-century brick one within an 1800s sandstone box plus a mansard roof and a Bavarian spire. This character seems reflected in a later owner, that extraordinary lucky soldier of fortune, Viscount Beresford, who in 1806 led an unauthorized expedition escorted by equally illegal warships against the Spanish colony of La Plata. He took Buenos Aires, the capital, in 1806, but not for long because the people rose against him and forced him to surrender. Beresford was interned amid the wild life and cattle of the Pampa where he and his officers fished, hunted and played cricket. This defeat was followed by an even worse one the next year, 1807, for reinforcements arrived from England under General Whitlocke; in one day the British Army lost over 400 killed, 650 wounded and 2,000 taken prisoner. These two victories by the citizens of Buenos Aires ran throughout Latin America, and began the overthrow of Spanish rule. They are rarely mentioned in British history books, but the Argentines remember them—as I discovered when teaching in that country. Beresford continued his lucky escapes in the Peninsular campaign, but Wellington said of him, "he alone could feed an army", and in an arid and devastated land like Spain perhaps this was more important than his fighting ability.

Before we leave the Tee, downstream are two typical but totally contrasting Kentish houses. One is the well-known, half-timbered 1470 manor house of Pattenden, the other an unknown and simple tile-hung house called the "Glen", but in a delightful riverside setting.

Goudhurst is a town with such fine views that it has been said that if Kent is the garden of England then Goudhurst is the garden of Kent. Its hilly High Street contains some fine pubs like "The Vine", "Eight Bells" and the "Star and Eagle", and Flemish weavers lived here for three centuries. St Mary's Church with its massive tower is inside mostly a Culpeper shrine, for there are memorials to four generations, seen all the better because of the clear glass, the older stained glass having been destroyed in 1940. Outside are the preserved cottages of Churchyard Row all adding to the visual delight that this small town presents to the beholder.

The Teise below now bends north and begins its long lower course to the Medway. The sharp bend here is an "elbow of capture", for in former times the Upper Teise flowed eastwards to join the river Rother in Sussex, and the Lower Teise cut back southwards into the soft Weald clay and captured it.

Not far away is St Margaret's Church, Horsmonden—at least two miles from the village in a setting of parkland and hop-gardens; ironically the village church of All Saints became redundant, and is now a Catholic church. The best part of the village is undoubtedly the large and beautiful Furnace Pond, whose important ironworks were run by John Browne, being conveniently near to the Medway, with an easier route via the Thames. Whilst trying to walk round this sheet of water with its overhanging trees, I wandered into a neighbouring hop field which had a short sharp notice: Keep out—Hop wilt! This is a fungoid disease easily carried by walkers, so I literally "hopped it"; after all, I am a beer drinker too!

North of Horsmonden the Teise divides into two natural chan-nels, both meandering across the Low Weald through willows, orchards and hops, a countryside best seen in springtime with blossom, fleecy clouds and lambs. The easterly branch, known sometimes as the Twist, nearly became a canal, when during the Napoleonic Wars the sea routes were hazardous and Rennie revived an earlier scheme; but the frightful cost and construc-tion problems stifled it completely. The Twist flows near Marden, a pleasant enough but rather expanded town on the main railway to Folkestone, and then it joins the Beult near Hunton. The Teise itself continues placidly to Laddingford, with its old small two-arched bridge and fifteenth-century weather-boarded pub, to join the Medway at Twyford Bridge.

The Beult (pronounced Belt) is the longest Medway tributary and virtually drains the great clay plain of the Kentish Weald, although it is not all clay as within it are sandstone and shelly limestone bands. This last occurs around Bethersden and is known as Bethersden Marble, but it is not unique to Kent for it is also known as Petworth or Sussex Marble. However, many Kent churches are embellished with it, and it takes a high polish. These variations in rock can be seen by looking at the twists and turns of the river's course, where it has etched its valley along the weaker bands.

The Beult was the third of William Lambarde's Medway "brooks". He considered its rise to be at "Goldwel in Great

Charte". Its source is about half a mile west of Great Chart church. This is an interesting building, which has a medieval bell inscribed "Sum Rosa Pastia Munda Maria Vocat" (I am Virgin Mary the ringing rose). Inside is the memorial to Nicholas Toke, of the local "big family", who died in 1605, had five wives and was the last knight to be buried in full armour.

The Beult virtually rises underground in the Hythe limestone beds ridge and flows out through a curious brick arch into a ditch and under the A28 road to reappear near and around Moat House further along. This is one of a number of curiously moated buildings at this end of the Weald. Although the flow appears insignificant it supplied water for centuries to Court Lodge Farm alongside Great Chart church. This is a very large building with a fine tall roof with blackened timbers inside from the fires in the original hall; part of the building dates from 1290. The river pursues a meandering course to near Pluckley station and then joins southerly branches from Bethersden of marble (and Colt cedarwood houses) fame and High Halden which join the stream at Vesperhawk Farm near Smarden and make a real river of it.

Smarden has been described as the perfect village, which presents problems of description. What is it then that makes it so attractive to us modern town-bred travellers? Firstly, surely, is its compactness; it has no sprawl, which is a rare attribute today; next, it has a really fine church; thirdly, it has many good houses of great variety: half-timbered, weather-boarded and tile-hung; and lastly, but certainly equally meritorious, its fifteenth-century bridge over the Beult. The only flaw in all this is the traffic that sometimes threatens life and limb on the B2077 from Charing and Biddenden.

St Michael's Church is built of mixed materials as well as architectural styles (fourteenth and fifteenth century): limestone rubble, fawn Bethersden marble and Kentish rag, but it is none the worse for that. Inside is vast, barn-like and severely simple, a very impressive interior with lots of fine timberwork and strange but interesting windows.

Smarden houses are almost beyond description. Many of the best have connections with the cloth trade and Flemish families. In Water Lane stands the Cloth Hall of about 1430, originally a farmhouse but altered to a warehouse complete with hoist and loft. In the main street is a Flemish family house dating back to 1331 complete with weaving shed behind; it belonged to the Pells and is called Dragon House. And one could go on, but an

early fifteenth-century house just up from the splendid Chequers
Inn intrigued me; as with an old forge used for a showroom of
beautiful objects, it belonged to a mother and daughter who run
an antique furniture business. The daughter sat outside in the
sunshine expertly recovering a chair; she fitted the main street
perfectly, for modern Smarden is a small craft centre.

It is a sad reflection on what the twentieth century has done to
Kentish villages to realize that Walter Jerrold in his *Highways
and Byways in Kent* of 1907 and 1924 makes virtually no mention of Smarden's glories. I can only suppose that there must
have been many more villages or houses equal to or maybe even
better than Smarden that have long ceased to be worthy.

From Smarden the Beult flows north west towards Headcorn
with the river well away from roads in its long sluggish middle
course. It then swings south of Headcorn, a town very definitely
in two parts. From its eastern approach you could be forgiven for
thinking it had no history, but in fact it was a seventh- or
eighth-century "den" clearing for pannage. In 1934 a Neolithic
polished axe was found in the river, which suggests an entry
into the Weald for hunting. The old centre is around the church
of St Peter and St Paul with its avenue of chestnuts planted at
Queen Victoria's Diamond Jubilee in 1898. It was built by a
Culpeper in the late fourteenth century of Bethersden marble
and ragstone quoins. Inside like Smarden, there is a fine timber
roof with close-set rafters reflecting the quantity of good oak in
the Wealden forests. Outside is a battered old remnant of this
forest, the famous Headcorn oak, which may be 900 years old as
it is connected with an ancient altar stone, and might be a
"Gospel Oak".

Headcorn was a cloth town with two Cloth Halls, and this is
also evident with the weaving cottages along Church Walk on
the north side of the church. These are a splendid row with all
sorts of styles, hung tiles, timber and plaster and weather-board-
ing, but all blend beautifully. An interesting pub, opposite the
Cloth Hall in the High Street, was the haunt of "free traders",
i.e. smugglers, and is called the "Kings Arms"; but if you look
closely it is the white cockade of the Jacobites that appears on
the Royal Arms.

The cloth trade eventually languished and Headcorn slept
until the coming of the railway to the Weald in 1842. It is
difficult to realize fully the change that took place, for the Weald
until then had been almost as impenetrable for the people of
Headcorn as it had been for the Domesday Commissioners eight

centuries earlier. The railway history of the town is quite interesting, as at the beginning it was for a few months the actual
end of the line with stage-coach connection to Folkestone. In
1905 the Kent & East Sussex Light Railway arrived full of
ambition from Robertsbridge, but the little railway was always
penurious and under the shadow of its owner and engineer,
Lieutenant-Colonel Stephens, who discouraged enthusiasm.
The last war, however, gave it a boost for it was strategically
useful, and carried the pipeline "Pluto", heavy rail-mounted
guns and vital food supplies. Eventually Dr Beeching admin-
istered the final anaesthetic in 1961, but at the southern end
from Tenterden a small section has reawakened and is operated
with enthusiasm as a vintage railway. In 1940 Headcorn had
the job of feeding the troops after Dunkirk, when a hundred
trains per day stopped for just eight minutes; beef was roasted
on spits in trenches near the line and one million sardines were
consumed.

The Beult west of Headcorn is joined by the river Sherway,
whose source is high up on the scarp slope of the Greensand
Ridge. On this stream is Coldbridge Farm, built of ragstone and
sited above a moat where once a triangular castle stood. The
origin of its shape is mysterious; it was built in the reign of
Edward I by Fulce de Peyforer, the King's escheator, or control-
ler, of lands that passed to the Crown. I went to see this farm,
which is delightfully old-fashioned with great crowds of fowl,
ducks and geese (more like a Normandy farmyard) milling
about and enjoying the moat fed from the Sherway. Whilst
talking to Mrs Hope, the farmer's wife, about its history one of
the many farm cats—a small one—marched past dragging a
large rabbit, a rural scene more of the past than the present.

Near where the Sherway joins the Beult at Wheeler's Street is
a curious three-level road, rail and stream bridge; part of it has
been recently rebuilt, but it remains much as it was when
ingeniously constructed in 1840 by the old South Eastern Railway. Downstream from the Sherway confluence the Hammer
stream enters; apparently its name is not derived from ironworking but from an old English word for bird, possibly *hama*
(feathers) hence: yellowhammer, but its origin is misty.

The stream's most interesting feature is that the headwaters
feed the lake and moat in the grounds of Sissinghurst Castle,
better known for the fine gardens created by Vita Sackville-
West. The building, however, once looked like Ightham Mote did
around 1400; it was later demolished by Sir John Baker, Queen

Mary's Chancellor, better known as "Bloody Baker" because of his anti-Protestant activities. He built the present castle in 1550, but its subsequent history was very mixed having been a prisoner-of-war camp for the French captured during the Seven Years War (1762) and in the nineteenth century was almost a complete ruin.

The great Tudor mansion was in 1930 rescued from oblivion by two talented people: Vita Sackville-West and Harold Nicolson. Ironically Vita Sackville-West returned to the seat of her ancestors for she was a direct descendant of "Bloody" Baker whose daughter had married Thomas Sackville, 1st Earl of Dorset. Some years ago my wife's mother whilst visiting Sissinghurst saw her gardening, a tall thin lady of determined aspect in the midst of "profusion . . . within the lines of utmost linear severity", as she described her gardens. I saw Sissinghurst on what had been a sunny warm day in May, although by the time I reached there the weather had changed and I walked in lonely state round the gardens and later the lake. I felt an atmosphere of profound melancholy heightened by later seeing Vita Sackville-West's own room in the Gatehouse tower; in spite of these fine gardens there is an air of sadness stretching back for centuries. In 1964 the Treasury accepted Sissinghurst as part payment for estate duty from the Nicholson family; compulsory self-destruction of British heritage by the imposition of death duties was avoided by the National Trust.

Coming back to the Beult, a river of many bridges, a small two-arched old stone bridge carries the Frittenden road over the river from Headcorn. This is Stephen's Bridge, named after Archbishop Stephen Langton who built it in the thirteenth century primarily so that he could travel more easily between his manors at Charing and Teynham to his estates at Slindon in Sussex—but it helped in the development of Headcorn, focussing upon the town the well-trod trackways in the confused and formless clay landscape.

The Beult is still a clean river, and one result of this is the survival of the rarer varieties of water plants especially between Headcorn and Staplehurst. The tall yellow flowers of the Greater Spearwort (*Ranunculus lingua*) are sometimes seen, a species of buttercup which grows best in water. In sheltered reaches the bright pink of the flowering rush (*Butomus umbellatus*) and the white flowers with a large purple spot of the Arrowhead (*Sagittaria sagittifolia*) decorate the river.

The river winds on under the main railway line to Ashford,

then flows north again near Spills Hill Farm. The railway bridge here over the river is a descendant of the one involved in the Staplehurst accident of 9th June 1865 on the S.E.R., an accident which was disastrous, curious and famous. Disastrous for it was the worst in the company's history with ten killed, fifty injured and eight coaches falling into the river Beult. Curious because sections of the actual running rail had been removed to repair the bridge and the District Inspector and Foreman Plate-layer had forgotten that the tidal boat express from Folkestone was due. Tidal because the service varied according to the Chan-nel tides (they mistook the day!); these trains lasted until 1885. Famous because Charles Dickens was a passenger returning from France. He escaped unhurt and helped with the injured and mentions the accident later in his preface to *Our Mutual Friend*. The railway acted quickly, the General Manager, F. W. Eborall, taking a locomotive from Tonbridge and going in per-son to the scene.

Staplehurst station doesn't seem to have had much luck either, for it was bombed during the war and caught fire im-mediately after it had been repaired. The town itself today hardly merits mention, having been swamped by suburban housing, far too much and quite unsuited for such a small centre. When I see it and the east end of Headcorn, I sometimes regret the Kent Coast electrification which has unwittingly spoilt towns and made a pleasant mode of travel into a daily rat-race.

The Beult now flows north-west through an area where bridges and causeways appeared early, for it was marshy ground and the unregulated river often flooded over its banks and water meadows. Stile Bridge, which now carries the A229 Hastings road, was a causeway—virtually an old stone embankment—and was one of the reasons why the proposed canals and navi-gation schemes often came to naught as the cost of rebuilding to take waterborne traffic was fearful.

At length the Beult passes through the hop-gardens of Hun-ton, south of the moated manor house of Hunton Court and picks up the Twist, passes the weir of the old water mill and enters Yalding. This is still a very attractive little waterside town with a seven-arch medieval stone causeway bridge spanning the two wide channels of the river; not all the arches are of the same age, however. Its narrowness clogs the commuter traffic at times, but to widen it would be sheer vandalism in a town like this for the character of Yalding is very much reflected in its buildings. And

these are all distinctive with the onion-shaped top to the thirteenth-century tower of St Peter and St Paul's Church; the
Woolpack and Swan Inns (the latter having a cellar in one of the
bridge arches); several old timber-framed houses and some
splendid Georgian houses with tall windows and dormers in the
High Street and opposite the church a farm with oasts. Finally,
Yalding Lees, a fine expanse of common land, fills the space
between the confluence of the Beult and Medway making a rare
open approach to the town, and a pleasant backwater stretch of
river scenery.

9

The Middle Medway—Yalding to Maidstone

From Yalding eastwards the valley of the Medway changes as the river, now increased by the waters of the Teise and Beult, cuts its gap through the Greensand Ridge.

However, the richness and fertility of the valley increases, as the geology changes and limey sands and clays are added to the rich deposits of past river flow and ice ages. The result of all this is verdant meadows flanking slopes covered with orchards and hop-gardens. In 1823 William Cobbett, who admired cultivated land above all else, remarked on one of his Rural Rides: "From Maidstone to Merryworth is about 7 miles, and these are the finest seven miles that I have ever seen . . ."

These cultivated slopes are on the Hythe beds of limestone from which were quarried the famous hard blue-grey Kentish rag building stone. Throughout the centuries this was expertly used by the Romans and Normans, and later by the Kentish masons (until the arrival of the cheap mass-fired brick). But ragstone still paves Kentish roads and is used as a filler for river, road and railway earthworks.

From Twyford the old navigation canal "cut" avoiding the large river bend at Yalding follows closely a length of main road, called Hampstead Lane, to Hampstead Lock near Yalding station. This proved to be a very expensive piece of road indeed for the old Medway Company, as they neglected to look after it, and the County who about eighty years ago assumed the charge of the roads sued them and won to the tune of £3,000. The railway runs along the left bank from Yalding right through Maidstone to Strood, and is a very good way to see the river which flows through the changing rural, urban, industrial and tidal landscape on its way to the sea.

Away up the slopes beyond the Iron Age hill fort of Nettle-stead is the imposing red-brick Elizabethan mansion of Roydon Hall where Sir Roger Twysden lived, but like so many we have passed it no longer belongs to the family. Sir Roger presented the famous Kentish Petition of 1642 which was a typical act of righteous solid protest by Anglican country gentry against the arbitrary actions of a Puritan parliament towards the Church and control of the militia. Parliament reacted sharply and

arrested Twysden and the other leaders, and this in turn caused
the petitioners to become more extreme and after an assembly
on Blackheath of many thousands there were many more
arrests. These events virtually made Civil War inevitable.
Apart from all these happenings Sir Roger Twysden was a
famous scholar and antiquary and a member of a group of
Kentish scholars that have been described as forming almost a
"dispersed university".

The river at Hampstead is a very pleasant spot at which to
linger; afterwards the towpath goes on by high banks with
willows to Nettlestead, whose name—apt enough but rather too
simple—was said to mean "valley of nettles", for there are
plenty of them about. However, it is more likely a personal
name from "Nede's stead" or "Nede's place". Still, it is an interesting little place both in fiction and fact, for it was here that C.
Northcote Parkinson in his fictional biography of Admiral Lord
Hornblower decided that Hornblower's house "Smallbridge
Manor" was sited. He put it west of the present B2015 road and
says "it was therefore on the branch line from Paddock Wood at
some point between Nettlestead and Wateringbury...the smoke
from the passing locomotives being visible from the upper windows of the house . . ." He goes on to say that the Admiral was
"provided with good neighbours at Mereworth Castle and Roydon Hall". It was very conveniently burnt down in 1884—by
Parkinson.

However, these fictional events seemed so life-like to many
readers that Parkinson once had a letter from a Nettlestead
churchwarden saying that the people of the parish were troubled
by pilgrims demanding to see the Admiral's tomb and the memorial tablet in the church! I met Mr Allen, a churchwarden of
Nettlestead House, Nettlestead Green, who remembered these
visitors very well, and he added that they often went away
convinced that the people of Nettlestead were hiding something. Which goes to prove, I suppose, that fiction can often be
more convincing than fact.

Leaving fictional history now for the real thing, the small and
ancient church of St Mary next door to Nettlestead Place up on
the bank from the river is a rather unusual building. The tower,
tiled and thirteenth century, is a survivor from an earlier
church, but the present nave has six enormous windows built
about 1420 onwards by Reginald de Pympe, Lord of the Manor
next door. They were filled with stained glass of the period and
their subsequent history was one of destruction, for during the

Reformation iconoclasts smashed the east window; this glass depicted the Crucifixion and the Virgin Mary, and were unpopular subjects with these latter-day vandals. And during the Great Storm of August 1763 the windows on the south side were destroyed by hailstones.

The Scott family succeeded the Pympes at Nettlestead Place and one of them, Edward, a Parliamentarian, achieved dubious fame by besieging his Royalist wife for four days in the house.

From the churchyard a very fine fourteenth-century gateway leads to the house and grounds with terraces and ponds; these gardens in times past were much larger and swept unbroken down to the river. When the river level falls stones are revealed, which suggests that there may have been a ford here. Parkinson used this historical possibility to create a fictional bridge, the origin of his "Smallbridge Manor", which shows the research put into his ingenious book.

Nettlestead Place was in a rather poor condition until 1922 when it was restored; it is still impressive, though it depends on where you view it from, for it is an incongruous arrangement of a Tudor banqueting hall flanked on one side by oast kilns. The building is now flats, and has an uncared-for appearance with the usual modern domestic clutter.

Along the road towards Wateringbury is Cherry Hill vineyard planted in 1966 and thus the first commercial one in Kent since the Reformation. The site is an old cherry orchard, and is interesting because it is near one of the several Roman vineyards of the second century in the Medway valley. The wine is actually made at Lamberhurst and called Kentish Sovereign, and I have tasted several bottles of the '76 vintage, which was an outstanding year for northern vineyards and here was no exception.

From Cherry Hill by winding lanes and round the back of Roydon Hall you come at length to the very cosily situated village of West Peckham in a rural cul-de-sac. This is quite a different village from its East namesake, and has a fine traditional green beside a church with a Norman tower. Inside is a curious upper room above the nave for the local gentry, in this case the Geary family from Oxon Hoath. The land round about used to be a soft-fruit region for I remember large fields of raspberry canes not long back among the orchards.

North of here down a long lane in an area known as Peckham Hurst on the slopes below Mereworth Woods is our smallest Medway vineyard called Littlefield. The owner, Mr Taylor, a Thames river pilot, shows the typical great enthusiasm that the new English vignerons are putting into this revival of an ancient pursuit. With cheerful confidence he showed me his 1½-acre (0.6 hectare) sheltered well-sited plot which has fine views over the distant Medway; its only disadvantage, it seems, is its size. Mr Taylor had no doubts about the future of English white wine, although he admitted it was a specialist market, and for slopes like his you really need small vineyard tractors which are expensive.

Having now seen all the Medway valley vineyards I began to reflect upon their future which depends on two main factors: price and climate. The first for all commercial growers—large and small—is hampered by the ridiculous duty imposed upon wine. As all British governments refuse to do anything about this, the E.E.C. currently is endeavouring to reduce *all* duty on wine, which is far too high in some countries in the E.E.C. The climate factor is often ignored, but it is certain that we are in a decline following the warm period of our grandparents (roughly 1900 to 1950), and little sun and a late vintage is the future prospect for English vignerons. It will of course affect, and is affecting, all northern vineyards—the Mosel, Rhine and Champagne region—so good English white wine may have a rarity value in the future. As a wine drinker and not a connoisseur I shall hardly be able to afford it and my attitude is probably best summarized by Lord Byron's Don Juan:

> If Britain mourns her bleakness, we can tell her, the very best of vineyards is the cellar.

Between West Peckham and Mereworth, well seen on the gently rising ground from the road, is the attractive Caroline brick house of Yotes Court, built in 1658 (during the Commonwealth). Country houses in Kent of that period are now rare and Yotes Court is the only complete surviving example. It now stands as built with the smaller upper windows and mullions and chimneys restored to their original state. The manor site is old, and Hasted (the Kentish historian) traced it back to Edward III. There have been many owners and it became the property of James Master who bought it from his stepfather Sir Thomas Walsingham in 1651. He built the new house around the earlier Tudor one and now the effect of a hipped roof, dormers and tall chimneys is very pleasing to the eye. Next door are the stables, a restrained but pleasant building of the same period—one may wonder here why modern buildings for utilitarian purposes can't be likewise. The house at length became the property of Viscount Torrington (the same family as the ill-fated Admiral Byng, shot on his own quarter-deck in 1757, of whom Voltaire remarked that the English shoot an admiral from time to time *"pour encourager les autres"*). This family held Yotes Court until 1948, and in 1951 it became the property of Mr and Mrs Mackay, by whose great kindness I was shown all over the building and grounds.

Inside the ceilings are outstanding, the first being the painted one over the staircase (done in the 1740s and believed to be by Francis Hayman, 1708-76; the staircase itself is superb with its fine balusters. The next ceiling of note (which I found intriguing because of its material) is the papier-mâché one with floral motifs in the south bedroom. The other fine ceiling, this time plaster ornamented, is in the long hall which runs through the middle front of the house. Upstairs in a smaller bedroom Mrs Mackay pointed out the bust of Queen Victoria given as her usual gift to her hosts wherever she stayed. The grounds are wide and embracing, and in a corner Mr Mackay showed me a tulip tree he had planted—a delight for a future owner to behold. On the north side is a large and fine kitchen garden, and on the east side is some Kentish rag walling. The house is built on a west-east slope which was used to gain an extra storey on the east side which forms a kind of undercroft. Mrs Mackay, who is an archaeologist, showed me the interesting rooms and walling that this makes, and thought that there are still mysteries about the former house to solve. I came away from here feeling that this house was in good hands, and that the cheerful atmosphere prevailing there would only be maintained by a private family and not an institution of any kind—however worthy.

Eastwards from the house lies Mereworth, a village that has plenty to see within its bounds. The name is a personal one from Meera's homestead ("worth"). At Mere House belonging to Maidstone's M.P. John Wells, a horticulturalist, there are gardens open in spring and summer, which are a quite delightful homely mixture of a long reedy lake, many good trees including larches, sycamores and a Blue Cedar with fine lawns and arum lilies among the potatoes. If you're lucky enough to meet Mrs Wells, she will explain it all very nicely.

Further along is the church of St Lawrence, built about the time of the 1745 Jacobite rising, and completely different from any other in Kent. Its appearance is suggestive of the well-known St Martin-in-the-Fields, in London, especially the steeple. This is bold and conspicuous, being a square tower. Within it is the belfry, on which is a lantern circled by Ionic columns; above them is a balustrade out of which arises the octagonal spire—a beautiful and impressive landmark. Below the roof with its enormous eaves is a fine curved porch supported by Tuscan pillars. The inside is arranged clearly and simply with two lines of painted Doric columns (to look like marble); and has a spaciousness which would have been more marked in its first hundred years when there were no pews. Two monuments are of special interest; the rare heart shrine of the Nevill family in the chapel brought from the old church; and in the vestry the memorial to Rear-Admiral Lucas (1834-1914), the first man to win a V.C.—gained in the Baltic in 1854-5. This very interesting, fine church sets us an intriguing mystery, for nobody knows who the architect was.

At the other end, off the main road, is Mereworth Castle, sometimes disparaged, mostly by those who can't get inside to see it; but I think it is one of the most splendid buildings in Kent. It is essentially an English adaptation of a Palladian villa built by Colen Campbell for John Fane, 7th Earl of Westmoreland in 1723. If you go to Vicenza in Italy you will see the Villa Capra built for Palladio for Paolo Americo, a town official; this was the model for Mereworth to be built by a Scottish architect who had never seen Italy.

It might be said, then, that Mereworth descends from an Imperial Roman villa by way of the Italian Renaissance to Palladian ideas transplanted in England. This means, briefly, that the house is a dome topped by a lantern on a large square building with four porticos having classical pediments and, on the north and south sides, flights of steps as well. It is a beautifully symmetrical building sitting in the Medway valley as comfortably as it would in the Venetian plain. Inside, the dome makes a magnificent circular hall, with golden panelled rooms that have paintings and tapestries and a very long beautiful drawing-room runs along the south front. Upstairs, reached by a spiral staircase, there is a glass gallery. But Mereworth is no showcase for it is a comfortable house to live in with such things as a lift and billiard rooms.

The modern history of the house is exciting, for this regal building was the setting for the film of Ian Fleming's *Casino Royale*, where James Bond plays baccarat for enormous stakes to outwit a shadowy character who uses his gains for sinister projects. The present owner is His Excellency Sáyed Mohamed

Mahdi-al-Tajir, an oil baron and ambassador in London for the United Arab Emirates, who broke the bank to buy it and James Bond's ghost for over half a million pounds. But at least he opens the grounds to the public in June, which saves people like me from trespassing—for I have walked all round it, including the overgrown bramble and nettle entrance by the ruined triumphal arch.

One mysterious object I discovered was some ruined brickwork, which I later learnt was an ice house. These were introduced by Charles II and were the ancestors of ice boxes, refrigerators and deep freezes. They had to have three essentials: to be near a stream or pond, to be well insulated, and to have good bottom drainage when some of the ice thawed.

After the splendours of Mereworth, the straggling village of Wateringbury along the A26 road with its traffic may seem rather ordinary, but the road southwards towards the river has a Whitbreads brewery and a church which looks rather grim but inside is interesting. It contains a very famous and much-written about piece of blackened wood with a fearsome spike, for prising open doors, which is known as the Dumb Borsholder of Chart, because it was the stand-in for the official (Borsholder— from *borhes ealdor*, borough's head) who policed the manor. In reality a deputy was elected by fee-paying householders; the last holder was a famous blacksmith, Thomas Clampard, who died in 1748. His epitaph almost seems to be a standard production for it appears on forty or more stones up and down the country. Indeed, in a book called the *Iron Horse* (Firth, 1892), I read of an adaptation of the same verse referring to an engine driver who died in 1840, and describing his locomotive: "no water does my boiler fill, but lying cold and still—shunted". Another monument is to Sir Oliver Style, a Sheriff of London in Jacobean times, the sole survivor of a large dinner party in Smyrna, Turkey, when the last course was an earthquake.

The brewery dates from about 1820 and has some fine chestnut trees, but little remains of the original building which was owned by the Leney brothers and drew its water from springs and wells—not the Medway, although all the materials came in by barge. Jude, Hanbury & Company, later owners, were blending their own whisky in 1860, and then the firm moved to Canterbury in anticipation (of all things) of the Channel Tunnel —shades of our own dashed hopes! The building was burnt in 1904, hence the Phoenix sign still used, and in 1930 Whitbreads bought it, maintaining their policy of keeping old established businesses going. Since 1950 brewing has been specialized for the export of beers like barley wine. For those who feel that the E.E.C. hasn't risen to their expectations, brewing flourishes mightily, and Whitbreads and Stella Artois in Belgium have a long, amicable and profitable relationship. Although I couldn't taste any of their export products, the kind and helpful manager gave me a good cup of tea.

Riverside Wateringbury is quite picturesque—the name aptly enough is from Wotringberia, a low and watery site—but as I walked about in the sunshine I thought it was rather spoilt by too many pleasure craft, clutter of buildings and fenced-off moorings. Suddenly I was shaken to hear my thoughts being echoed aloud by a youngish Cockney who had known the area in her childhood as a hop picker, and was apparently outraged at what it had become! Along the valley nearer to Teston the traffic noise becomes intrusive, in contrast to the railway whose noise is intermittent. In steam days it brought many anglers from Paddock Wood for the reach here is popular with fishermen whose large green umbrellas dot the banks in all sorts of weathers under which they sit unconcerned, patient and eternally hopeful.

Soon comes Teston Lock and the beautiful medieval six-arched bridge. This place was once a litter black-spot and the waterside plants on the bank were often damaged, but now there is a nicely landscaped amenity area with car park and bins—a great improvement. The bridge is very narrow with massive cutwaters from the time when it had to withstand flooding before the river had been locked and regulated. Over a century ago three arches were rebuilt, but so carefully that it cannot be noticed. There exists a very fine painting of the bridge viewed from the west by that master of the Kentish landscape, Rowland Hilder; it is a scene almost unchanged in time.

Teston village is not now particularly attractive, but it does contain the other half of the cricket-ball making craft at the Invicta Works of Alfred Reader. Its history is long, interesting and complex; for those who demand detail you cannot beat Hugh Barty-King's book, *Quilt Winders and Pod-Shavers*. I was made a very welcome visitor here by Leslie Adams, one of the directors, and it was a great pleasure to see this craft flourishing in spite of economic difficulties. Here at Teston the basic craft processes are similar to Chiddingstone, although there are some differences. They still employ directly twenty-two craftsmen, but they have pioneered a ball that more than complies with the

M.C.C. optimum "bounce" (35 per cent). In this they have moved away somewhat from the original quilted-cork centre and made one that is hand-wrapped cork laminations, rubber and Terylene fibre, cured under great pressure and then fitted with leather covers and hand-stitched in the traditional way by their craftsmen.

The firm diversified a great deal and today they make cricket balls of many types: rubber covered, hollow and plastic. An enormous number of hockey balls are also produced for an important European market (Germany, Holland and Belgium), as well as being sent overseas to Japan, Australasia and South Africa. Mr Adams thought that the hand-made balls were still under-priced, but the whole process gave immense job satisfaction. One can only echo this, and long may they reign.

From Teston a side road goes to East Malling—hardly a village now for it's really almost a fingertip of one of Maidstone's suburban fists poking across the Kentish countryside. But here is Bradbourne House, for nearly 300 years a home of the cadet branch of the Twysden family, established in the Restoration; together with its large estate, it is now a famous Agricultural Research Station doing valuable work on fruit—tree, bush and cane—and keeping a large area still green. Until recently the land around East Malling was a massive cherry-growing area, but this delectable fruit is now in decline. Cherry orchards seem to have many problems: large uneconomic trees, nobody (in spite of high unemployment) will pick the fruit, keeping off birds appears impossible as they ignore all kinds of expensive noise, and finally the trees take fifteen years to mature. Well, what did they do years ago? Why are the Italians so successful? How about a miniature cherry tree? Nobody seems to know or care!

Across the orchards is the town of West Malling in great contrast to its rather suburban brother. This is still a well-kept country town with a wide High Street and many fine houses (especially Georgian) in it like Arundel and Street Houses. Its spacious centre sets off the narrow streets and in Swan Street is St Mary's Abbey on the site of an old Benedictine nunnery founded by Bishop Gundolf of Rochester. The Norman tower and the fifteenth-century gatehouse survive alongside the modern chapel of the Anglican Benedictine Community; but its roof is undignified, the weak point of all modern buildings. The parish church is attractive enough with its mixed architecture, and the thirteenth-century chancel with its arches and sedilia as well as the curious medieval vestry are worth seeing. Southwards on the Mereworth road is the lovely, well-named Douces Manor, once a restaurant and now institutionalized; across the road is its beautiful long lake. Altogether West Malling is a fine little town and although somewhere there must be the usual uninspired mid-twentieth century expansion, you are not conscious of it.

Further along is the disused old and famous R.A.F. airfield, built on the sandy soil of East Malling Hoath, which Kent County Council recently acquired as a speculation—its future use has been suggested for executive jets. The locals, and I don't blame them, are anxious and cross because jets, however small, are noisy. To suggest its use for agriculture would merely be termed reactionary, but a research station for miniature cherry trees would at least be quiet.

Down a lane and side road leads to Offham with a very fine tidy well-kept village green. On it, near an outcrop of Kentish rag, is a quintain, a unique survivor of medieval or perhaps even Roman sport. This consists of a post with a swivel crosspiece at which you tilted on foot or mounted then tried to avoid the sandbag-like object hung at the other end, which if you weren't quick enough swung round and gave you a hearty wallop.

From Offham we come back again to Teston and its church, with the famous Nestor memorial of 1787 to a West Indian slave who was a faithful servant for twenty-two years to Dr James Ramsay (1733-89), a Naval chaplain, later the Rector of Teston, after having served on the West Indies station, and being distressed at what he saw there. I had a long talk with the present Rector, who like others has many parishes in his care—here West Farleigh and Wateringbury. He outlined very succinctly the Church's problem with its old buildings. He said that one received a building which is the focal point of heritage for the present as well as the future population. But how do you preserve it? In times past there had been many endowments, but here in spite of a congregation of 700, and income that ranged from £10,000 to £40,000, his church at Teston needed £80,000 spending on it—redundancy was therefore inevitable in the future.

Hard by the church is Barham Court, a house set in spacious grounds with an estate history going back to Norman times, when it was held by the Bearham family, originally known as Fitz Urse—son of a bear. Randolph Fitz Urse, or Barham, was one of the four knights responsible for the murder of Thomas à Becket, a deed which forced him to flee to Ireland. Later in 1634 the estate passed by marriage to the Boteler family from Bedfordshire. This was an interesting case of the gradual change within the Kentish gentry from the ancient custom of gavelkind (equally divided inheritance) to primogeniture (inheritance to the first born). It was considered that if the family property passed through a daughter in marriage, a new family was established. By contrast the independent middle-class Kentish yeomen maintained gavelkind much longer, for which we must be grateful as it has left Kent the heritage of many fine "Hall houses".

Teston is pronounced "Teeson". The reason for this is apparently due to the old South Eastern Railway, who employed a signwriter to make their station nameboard. He misspelt it and the company refused to alter it. The locals, however, continued to pronounce it as of old, although copying the "new" spelling of Teston. The station has now gone board and all, but its misspelt name lives on.

Over the river is West Farleigh with All Saints' Church tucked away from the main road with a mounting block still standing outside the parsonage. The church was originally Norman with a prominent fifteenth-century tower. So many churches in Kent have these later towers that it is thought they are additions in the years of recovery from the Black Death, which itself was largely caused by the climatic decline after the end of the medieval warm period. It was these climatic shocks producing famine and low resistance to the approaching Black Death, rather than the disease itself, which caused such havoc. The recovery in Kent was marked by the rise of the broadcloth industry producing surplus wealth, which meant that many parishes could rebuild or embellish their churches, as in East Anglia although not on the same scale.

After the church, westwards along the main right-bank road the B2010, is West Farleigh Hall, for long the *clou*, or chief attraction, of this hamlet. It is famous for its fine gardens, but I was lucky enough to be invited to have a look inside by the courtesy of the owner, Mrs Norman. It was built in 1719 and has the most beautiful brickwork—dull brown contrasting with vivid red—and mellowed walls, which always look right when they're old, but dreadful when new. Inside is a splendid two-storied hall, where a single Corinthian pillar supports the gallery and ceiling. This is a rare construction, but at Boston

Manor in the far south-west in Falmouth there is another example. There is a small but delightful library which is a lovely room.

Outside in the garden were herbaceous borders, which even I as a mere admirer realized were out of the ordinary. It was mid-July, and we were experiencing a dreadful damp and dismal summer, but these borders appeared as magnificent rectangles of solid colour: each separate—yellow, blue and white. Because the house is rather narrow the extent of the grounds seems considerable with a walk through the woods and even a picnic area.

Down a bridle path from the road junction with the B2163 lies Tutsham Hall and its orchards. After the Restoration in the 1660s two orchards of five acres were worth £2.40 an acre on the manor farm, although the whole unit of 223 acres (91 hectares) was worth less than £1 per acre. Such was the rising dominance of Kentish fruit farming, to last for over 250 years. Nowadays it seems that much modern fruit farming is uneconomic and expensive; but some of the growers haven't been very enterprising, have had a captive market for too long, and have been unable to withstand the cold blast of competition. Some of the facts may be unpalatable but they ought to be realized: too much reliance on the cold store, not enough replanting, and growing the wrong varieties of apples for a large distant urban market. In fact this highlights the whole problem of British farming. We are for better or worse an urban nation with a large industrialized population, and if farming and indeed the countryside are to survive it is perhaps time that farming was restructured, land tenure reviewed and farmers' banks established giving lower interest rates. The economic farming unit is the 70-acre (30-hectare) family farm, and much-vaunted talk of efficiency means little when less than 2 per cent of a huge population are on the land—with perhaps one member actually engaged in farming. Some of the younger unemployed ought to be encouraged to work on the land, not as labourers but rather as family farmers. Hop problems have been solved, so why not fruit? The apple barons and "agro-businessmen" have had their day, one feels.

Further along this bank is Kettle Corner where the hop-gardens sweep down to the river and the wooden Kettle bridge carries a by-road to East Barming. Older Ordnance Survey 1-inch maps used to show two Roman sites about half a mile apart on the left bank; the newer ones leave them out, which seems a pity for now there is no indication that they ever existed.

We are now in sight of what has been described as the finest bridge in the south of England. This is the medieval bridge at East Farleigh with its pointed arches and large solid cutwaters. This bridge had to contend with salt as well as fresh water, for here was the old tidal limit before the Allington Lock was built in 1792. Below the bridge is a lock, weir and modern sluices which see much summer activity with pleasure craft of all kinds with, usually, a lock-keeper to see that things don't become too lubbery. I was watching all this one day with an old waterman, and I heard him comment, "like a lot of sojers!", the supreme expression of disdain a sailor, fresh or salt, can make on clumsy boatwork.

East Farleigh is right in the hop belt with many oast kilns that have the later pyramid-type slate roofs and the gardens extend towards Maidstone, becoming a mass of green with their wires and strings in late summer. The valley from East Farleigh to Tovil has some interesting geology and history, for here are massive beds of Kentish rag which produced large quarries, especially in the Tovil area. Within these beds the local quarry-men discovered great fissures, some as much as 50 yards (46 metres) wide and ¼ mile (0.4 kilometres) long, which they termed "wents", and it was thought they were caused by huge torrents of water. Later research showed that they were really "gulls", that is: openings caused by cambering, a movement by the harder beds of limestone over the underlying thicker clays, and probably another legacy of the Ice Ages when the ground was frozen.

The Civil War here saw some typical Kentish activity, for a fierce battle at East Farleigh bridge marked the beginning of Kent's final assault against Parliament in 1648. The county's attitude towards Charles I had originally been a kind of conservative criticism, but in 1642, as we saw at the beginning of this chapter, came the famous Petition. In the years that followed Parliament took an increasing control of Kent—being far from the actual battlefields. Some in the county were suspicious of both Crown and Parliament, but after sequestration of estates and demands for men and money plus the exclusion of moderate Parliamentarians from the South-eastern Committee, anger mounted. The revolt was probably really more against "this thing called a Committee" than the Army and Parliament.

After a rousing meeting at Tunstall near Sittingbourne, the

rebels seized strategic points in East Kent including Walmer Castle, which so thoroughly alarmed Parliament that Sir Thomas Fairfax was sent with 8,000 men to repress the rising. He advanced from Blackheath towards Maidstone, and decided not to cross the Medway at Aylesford, but instead to advance south to East Farleigh Bridge where the heavily outnumbered Royalist defenders fought strongly, but were overcome. Fairfax then pushed on along the Tovil road towards the town, although his advance was fiercely contested all the way. The rest of the story concerns Maidstone and will be told in the next chapter.

The river route to Tovil is peaceful enough now, mainly because it is away from the roads, and there is a pleasant walk along the towpath below the orchards. On the river itself you can drift along under the overhanging Bydew Woods until you reach the industrial outskirts of the county town where the railway bridge to Tovil Paper Mills crosses the Medway. A notice here may shatter your illusions by reminding you that the river is dangerous as well as dirty, and that it could kill.

10

Maidstone and Its Rivers Medway, Loose and Len

The county town of Kent on the Medway, when seen for the first time, seems a large place—which it is indeed—but I am always surprised to learn that the population is around 70,000, for the centre is quite small.

Nevertheless, there is the usual rush and hurry of crowds, traffic and the inevitable boxlike glass and concrete buildings which are reducing all towns to what one used to read about in science fiction but now is a grim reality. Why then is this place the county town, instead of Canterbury or Rochester, both of ancient foundation and early centres of government, religion and trade? The answer is in its geography, which wasn't apparent until Kent was a county instead of a kingdom. Some 1900 years ago a Roman road from Rochester to Sussex passed through what is now Week Street, down Gabriel's Hill, crossed the river Len and went up Stone Street to become part of a road system of a sea-orientated iron industry. This route didn't make Maidstone a Roman town, but its surrounding fertile land did attract villas—and in a way perhaps was the very faint beginnings of a town to come.

Rome, however, was followed by the Dark Ages when town life everywhere became extinct and there were just rural settlements—not even villages. The Saxons later settled in compact villages, but even by Norman times towns were few. Domesday in 1086 records that whatever settlement was at "Meddestane" had a cluster of six water mills on its rivers.

The origin of the town's name is intriguing for there are many spellings and different meanings. "Maydenstan" (maiden's town), although attractive, now sounds fanciful as does "Meghanstone" (mighty stone town) and the real meaning may be from the river, "Medwegstan" (Medway's town), by reason of the slurred tongue of local speech. Its position on the river Medway where an east-west route crossed the river, whose fertile valley led to the Thames estuary and at the head of navigation, all contributed to Maidstone becoming the county town of Kent.

Religious fervour of the Middle Ages added to this importance in 1205 when the parish rector gave his manor house as a residence for the Archbishop of Canterbury, and later in 1395 Archbishop Courtenay established a collegiate church and a college for secular canons. All this medieval church activity has given Maidstone its finest group of buildings: the College, All Saints Church and the Archbishop's Palace built in the local ragstone on their splendid riverside site. The College suffered, as such places did, in the Dissolution of the Monasteries, passed to the Crown, had many owners, and now houses such diverse groups as Sea Cadets and a Music Centre within its gatehouses and hall.

The church is high and broad with a timber roof; it lost its timber spire in one of those many storms which seem to have damaged churches all over the Weald. The palace's history for a while depended upon the religious affiliations of the Crown: dissolution came with Henry VIII; it was restored to Cardinal Pole by Mary and finally disposed of by Edward VI; then followed many owners and at length it passed to Maidstone Corporation. Robert Goodsall once thought Maidstone didn't appreciate this building as much as, say, cities like Bruges and Ghent would if they had it, and knowing these last two places extremely well, I can't help but agree with him.

The river crossing is probably very old, but the bridge is much later, although by the fourteenth century a bridge existed, almost certainly built by the clergy—the only people who had the time, money and foresight to bridge rivers at that time. But the bridge confirmed Maidstone as the chief market town in mid-Kent, with the advantages of having carriers to London by road and water, for Maidstone was a port as well. The river became important for fishing, for the Mayor got powers in 1559 to control it from Hawkwood Stone (the boundary with Rochester) to East Farleigh (the tidal limit).

So now Maidstone, the county town with an important market, had to work for its living; but agriculture was dominant and the only industries then in Kent were ironworking way out in the Weald and clothing centred at Cranbrook. However, there was an offshoot of broadweaving in Maidstone, although the trade was changing to the lighter cloth or "New Draperies" pioneered in the Low Countries. As a result, in 1567 the town asked to be allowed sixty Dutch families and this in due course led to the thread-twisting industry which was to last for a century or so, and caused a new crop—flax—to be cultivated locally. By now the town was growing and from under 2,000 people in 1570 it had reached over 3,000 a hundred years later thus overtaking Rochester, although still way below Canterbury with 7,000.

We are now approaching the Civil War period and here I will take up the story again of the Kentish rising of 1648. Maidstone of course had been concerned in earlier risings, notably the Peasants' Revolt of 1381. This has been told often, and exploited for spurious motives by modern historians, when in actuality the real complaint was against high manorial rents.

Following Fairfax's assaults at East Farleigh, the Royalist General, Lord Goring, militarily not quite in the same class as Fairfax, directed 3,000 of his small force quartered at Penenden Heath into Maidstone. Fairfax after a terrific struggle at length reached Tovil, only to find that the river crossings of first the Loose and later the Len were to be met with even fiercer resistance. But the Royalists were gradually driven back up Gabriel's Hill and into the town centre where in St Faith's churchyard a last stand was made. Thus Maidstone fell to Parliament with heavy Royalist losses (1,400 prisoners; 300 dead and wounded); Lord Goring withdrew apparently towards London, but left men to defend Rochester Bridge. He then unexpectedly crossed the Thames at Greenwich to join a Royalist uprising in Essex, but 500 of Maidstone's defenders who also fought at Rochester later escaped to rejoin Goring. The Men of Kent were beaten, but their national aims expressed the wish of most Englishmen for a political settlement between Crown, Army and Parliament.

During the Commonwealth period, however, there was a strong Puritan preoccupation with the Devil and all his works, and in 1652 Maidstone was the scene of a famous witch trial (although witches have always been very rare in Kentish history, reputedly because of Roman and strong Christian influences). Six women were on trial, five from Cranbrook and one from Lenham, part of the evidence being a piece of "scorched meat" which the defendants claimed had been given to them by the Devil. This was exhibited at the "Swan" public house and in effect sent them all to the scaffold for "the execrable and diabolical crime of witchcraft". This might seem remote to you, but in very recent times a bewitched corn dolly made a local churchwarden very ill, and later his vicar too, so much so that exorcism had to be carried out by an Anglican priest, Dr Ormand.

We may picture the seventeenth-century town then as being built round the cross-roads pattern of the route from London via Wrotham and Ashford to Hythe over the original Roman road from Watling Street to the Channel. This formed four central streets: High, King, Week, Gabriel's Hill, with Earl Street, Mill Street and Pudding Lane leading off them. This is the town that Pepys would have seen in March 1669 when during his visit he saw flax being dressed in the street. And in 1724 when Daniel Defoe, that astute economic and social observer, visited the town he wrote: "From this town, and the neighbouring parts, London is supplied with more particulars than from any single market town in England..." He gave a long list including bullocks, timber, corn, hops, fruit, stone and sand. The last two items are interesting because the sand is the fine white variety from the local Folkestone Beds formation of the Lower Greensand which was then thought to be the best in England for making window glass, mirrors and for writing. And in fact this local product has continued to be used right up to the present day for moulding sand in casting metal. The chief cargo outwards from Maidstone by the Medway had always been Kentish rag (from the many quarries nearby), especially for street paving in London. But between 1674 and 1700 there was a rather special use of the stone when over 11,000 tons were transported for the rebuilding of St Paul's Cathedral by Wren following the Great Fire in 1666.

After 1740, as we saw earlier, the Medway upstream entered on a Golden Age, and downstream the Lower Medway Company in 1792 built Allington tidal lock and Maidstone became a barge-building town. By 1839 eleven firms were operating from the port, their tan-sailed barges carrying cargoes of paper and timber which was still being brought out of the Weald. The special narrow river barges known as "stumpies", some built in the Maidstone yards, were doing a roaring trade in bringing London's rubbish to Kentish brick kilns such as Snodland, where the raw material was the brickearth we mentioned earlier, the return cargoes being bricks.

By 1874 dozens of barges were threading their way through the maze of sailing traffic on the lower Medway at each tide, many heading for Maidstone. Steam appeared too in 1906 when the shallow-draught steamer *Pioneer* brought coal to Maidstone from Goole, but it failed to usher in a new waterborne age.

Gradually commercial river traffic has decayed and with it the industrial waterfront so now only a few barges or paper-pulp lighters from Bridge Mill linger on. One echo of this past in modern Maidstone is the converted industrial premises known as the "Warehouse", a sort of café-night club with live entertainment, frequented not by watermen but by Maidstone's youth bored perhaps with television and suburban life generally.

The food and drink industry in Maidstone has always been important, but in spite of being, as Defoe termed it, "Mother of Hop grounds in England", commercial brewing on a large scale was late in developing. This was because farms and many rural houses had their own brewhouses. Nevertheless, Maidstone finally became a brewing town, and for many years a familiar sight—and smell—were the three large breweries along the banks of the Medway. They are all gone now, more on account of discharging effluent into the river than anything else. But the town made other interesting drinks too, for a gin distillery flourished in Bank Street until 1825, and a true Kentish liqueur called Gazella was distilled as well. This was made from Gazles, an old Kentish name for blackcurrants. All this was the enterprise of George Bishop, Mayor in 1777 and again in 1786.

The nineteenth century saw a food revolution, many foods being processed into a manufactured product rather than made at home from basic raw materials—two of these made in Maidstone were custard powder and the famous Sharp's toffee; alas, this sticky schoolboy's delight is no longer made, its place taken by more sophisticated sweets.

The nineteenth century in Kent arouses associations with Dickens, but Maidstone which he knew well, and was much attracted to, figures very hazily in his novels. It is thought to have been his model for "Muggleton" in the famous cricket match in *The Pickwick Papers*, and there is a curious reference in *David Copperfield*. David is enquiring of the Dover boatmen as to the whereabouts of his Aunt Betsy Trotwood, and one of the answers was: "locked up in Maidstone Jail for child stealing"! This famous building in solid ragstone designed by David Alexander, who built the house in Mote Park, was mentioned to me once by a language teacher colleague of mine. Frustrated by her pupils' inactivity to grasp some first principles, she remarked to me "The spies I taught in Maidstone Jail were far more rewarding!"

Still, if Dickens didn't write about Maidstone he used the railway to the town a great deal. Although the South Eastern's branch from Paddock Wood came early (1844), and reached Strood twelve years later, the town was rather off the main lines. Even when the Chatham Company (L.C.D.R.) arrived in 1874, it was at first a single line, but it gave a quicker service to London than the S.E.R., making the through run from Maidstone East to Victoria in 75 minutes, which was not bad for that era.The same year the S.E.R. opened Maidstone Barracks station, a useful aid for a garrison town which was the home of the Royal West Kent Regiment, the old 50th Foot, known sometimes as the "Blind Half Hundred". Alas, they are no longer here, and in fact both Kent regiments are now combined, but the town still has the Royal Engineers who now occupy the barracks and other new buildings on the river bank.

The lines were electrified just before the war, and the railway rivalry of the nineteenth century had long-term results in providing strategic relief routes between London and the Kent coast in the conflict that followed. Here it may be added that in June 1944 Maidstone had the unique but unpleasant shock of being the most inland town in the world to be shelled by a coastal battery—a German position on the French coast.

The very advantage of Maidstone's position as a route centre for London, the Coast and the Weald made it in modern times a travail for through traffic, until the M20 by-pass was built. After hundreds of years of service the ancient Medway bridge was replaced in 1879 by a strong, handsome and solid Victorian structure by Bazalgette, the engineer who made the Thames Embankment; but even this had to be widened in 1926. Finally in 1978 a new modern concrete, but supremely graceful, St Peter's bridge was opened parallel to the older bridge, giving a much better traffic flow, and at the same time new landscaped gardens known as Jubilee Walk were made in the Queen's Jubilee Year. The whole effect is pleasing and impressive, and if they can improve the old Lockmeadow market area the town will have that natural focal point that all waterside towns should have.

The same cannot be said for the modern buildings; they are quite awful and seem to have been planned by a committee, designed by mathematicians and built by robots. One relieving feature exists in the Springfield complex, where there is a nice circular public library, and another is to be found at the top of the London Road where there is a group of elegant three-storey houses; good fenestration and height here have made all the difference.

But Maidstone has interesting buildings away from the main streets, for Bank Street of gin fame has some rare (for Kent) pargetting; there is also one house with it in Week Street, but it is engulfed by chrome and glass. Pudding Lane has some fine old houses and in St Faith's Street is an early nineteenth-century group of almshouses, and many of the minor streets and alleys are worth exploring; but you must walk them, preferably on early-closing day with fine dry weather.

The town does have two quite remarkable museums. The Town Museum is the old Chillington Manor House (sixteenth century) with the salvaged west wing of the Elizabethan timber Court Lodge at East Farleigh which was demolished in 1874. The inside was damaged by arsonists in 1977, but the collection is representative not only of Maidstone but also Kent, and the building contains the Art Gallery as well. The other one is the Tyrwhitt-Drake Carriage Museum inside the old Palace stables, another good ragstone building in Mill Street. Here is stabled a unique collection of animal-powered vehicles that might have been used by the inhabitants in Defoe's day when he remarked on "the gentlemen and persons of rank of both sexes, and some of quality" that you met at Maidstone. But there are humbler vehicles too, and this must form as a whole one of the most valuable fragments of history ever collected.

Maidstone if not mentioned in Dickens's fiction certainly appears in C. Northcote Parkinson's for it is the town of Admiral Lord Hornblower's forbears who were corn merchants and apothecaries, as well as the centre of operations for Hornblower when he was a captain in the "Sea Fencibles". These were a kind of coastal Home Guard, to repel French invaders, regarded with mixed feelings by naval officers. It was also where Hornblower's bank and solicitors had their premises—in the High Street.

The Medway has two tributaries that join the river at Maidstone, the Loose and the Len, both having played a large part in local life and the early days of water-powered industry.

The Loose is the most peculiar of the Medway's tributaries for it is one of those curious limestone streams that spend part of their life underground. This stream bubbles forth from a rock junction near Langley church of the Hythe Beds and the Atherfield Clay, and then flows into a reedy lake. It is not long in daylight for near the site of a Roman building it plunges down a swallow hole and flows through the limestone of the once prolific Boughton quarries, famous for their free-stone, but now no longer worked. Quarrying actually altered the Loose stream for it lowered the water table, and so it flows now lower than previously; it reappears just north of the great Iron Age hill fort at Boughton, a rather mysterious earthwork which is so large that it is thought it might have been some long-forgotten pre-historic hilltop town.

I was trying to trace this elusive stream on a drizzly St

George's Day, and near the quarry I met a timber merchant sitting in his own truck eating his lunch. Mr Edwards turned out to be quite a philosopher, and knew his local history as he remembered some of the former water mills on the Loose, and regretted the passing of Kentish rag to concrete, and said how much better Maidstone would have looked if they had continued to build in the local stone; he remembered some private houses built with it just before the war. This little river had sixteen mills along it at one time, and even in 1902 there were still six flour mills, two board and one paper mill working.

After Boughton it dives down again and comes up into a pretty valley with a small string of lakes before flowing through the village of Loose. The village is a pleasant watery place set in a steeply wooded valley, whilst far up above on a high bridge the Hastings Road traffic is out of sight and mind. This is not a typically Kentish village at all, for it looks as if it is one of the Oxfordshire villages on the Windrush in Cotswold limestone which has been placed in a Devon combe. One house in the village, a beautiful fifteenth-century half-timbered building, was completely restored nearly fifty years ago by the untiring efforts of Colonel Statham and left to the National Trust. Its interest lies in its name, Wool House, and was proof that the Loose was at one time a weaving river, not far from the main Kentish supply of fuller's earth at Boxley.

The valley now suddenly drops away down to the Medway, past former mills and ponds placed on the "knickpoints" or sharp breaks of slope in the valley. One of these is an old mill at Bockingford Steps; another is at Cisbrook Conservancy, now a wildfowl reserve with an old pump house that drew clean water for the paper mills. After this comes Hayle Mill, still working as a modern hand-made paper mill near Hayle Place, until the little river is finally submerged under the great paper-making mills of the Reed Group at Tovil. This started as a small fulling mill, changed to paper and was bought in 1894 and modernized by Albert E. Reed, a native of Cardiff who began his climb in the world of paper-making from very small beginnings.

The river Len is larger and longer than the Loose and begins in the hills south-west of the village that bears its name. Lenham has been described as a "failed" town, presumably because it didn't develop from its original grant to hold markets and fairs. The twentieth century has made up for it by dumping a huge freight depot off the A20 in Ham Lane, but it doesn't intrude—though of course you are aware of it. The "failed" town, however, has a nice central square with some fine buildings, which include the rebuilt fifteenth-century Saxon Warriors chemist's shop, where the skeletons of three armed sixth-century Saxons were found in 1948. Over the road are two pubs, "The Red Lion" and the weather-boarded "Dog and Bear"; next is a wine merchant in a small but delightful building, and finally the Douglas Almshouses.

Away from Lenham, the source of the Len is in Affers Wood on Runham Farm, now the property of Viscount Monckton of Brenchley. He kindly showed me the source spring spouting forth from a tangled tree-covered sandstone face on an early October day, after a futile search the previous April. The name Affers is thought to derive from a Jutish word for "heifers", and an ancient Jutish trackway leads across the farm to near the source. Viscount Monckton is something of an archaeologist and a diviner, who uses a whalebone "prong", which I thought twitched decisively in his hand; he said there might be a building below ground near the source (a shrine or a temple perhaps of a water goddess).

Later I saw the diggings of a recently excavated Romano-British villa, not as yet actually dated, and the excellent archaeological collection that Viscount Monckton has housed in an old farm building. There seems no doubt that on this farm was the site of continuous settlement stretching back to Lower Palaeolithic times, as calcined flints of that period have been found. An extraordinary collection of Roman objects excavated recently makes fascinating speculation: ancient German glass; the jaw of a Roman cow, Spanish amphora, Samian pottery from Lyons, a Syrian scent bottle, a Roman spring-loaded knife and a rare half-statue of a Roman Venus.

Below Runham Farm the Len enters a small lake that when I saw it was a great gathering point of wildfowl, and is soon joined by a brook from Harrietsham village now split by the A20. The southerly part is worth a walk round for it is rather unexpectedly made up of a variety of interesting buildings, outstanding being the sixteenth-century unrestored Old Bell Farmhouse with its jetty, which is considered the most complete Wealden House in Kent.

Over the road is a nice set of 1642 almshouses (rebuilt in 1770) and endowed by the Fishmongers Company. Up Rectory Lane is a 1632 house with its original chalk floor—for we are on the flanks of the Downs here—and next door is the Roman Catholic church of the Good Shepherd. This is a compact little building of wood and tiles, clear and light inside, which was originally an Anglican chapel for the railway workers building the old Chatham Company's branch line to Ashford from Maidstone in 1880-4.

After this little excursion, the river flows to Chegworth on a knickpoint where there is a restored mill house. At Broomfield the Len enters the grounds of Leeds Castle, a much advertised beautiful building now run by a charitable trust and used for conferences and medical seminars. The name is thought to derive from Led or Ledian, the chief minister of Kent's last king, Ethelbert IV, at the end of the Heptarchy or seven kingdoms in 857, so the nearby village became Esledes and hence Leeds. Little is known about the original wooden castle on the two islands rising from the marshes of the river Len which were later dammed to make a rather fine lake. The present impressive group of buildings that adorn the islands now are much rebuilt and restored from the original stone castle of 1119 by Robert de Crèvecour.

This was a typical strong Norman keep, and then followed another typical medieval adornment—a vineyard which flourished in the warm sunshine of Edward I's reign. In 1278 the castle passed to the Crown and was held by a succession of queens, and became somehow connected with the Culpepers; a later descendant, Lord Culpeper, actually Charles I's most trusted servant, became the owner. Of course Parliament sequestered it, but Charles II restored it to the family who leased it to the king for a prisoner-of-war camp, the custodian being none other than John Evelyn, the diarist.

Then came the Fairfaxes, and by the time the 7th Lord had it, the castle was dilapidated; he restored it to much as we see it now. Horace Walpole saw it in 1752 and damned it with faint praise, as he had done at Sissinghurst, Mereworth and Tonbridge. The succession of owners continued until finally the Hon. Lady Baillie bought it in 1926, and restored the furnishings also to what we see now.

Today the view as described by Lord Conway can be seen at close hand from a footpath that runs through the grounds close to the river. Thus I saw this beautiful castle on a fine early October day with fleecy clouds and its famous duckery inhabitants lined up like bathers at a pool. Out of the lake the Len waters feed the flow of the old castle millrace by the ruins of the mill that was one of thirteen at one time along the river's course; the waters rush down in a fine cascade to join the parent stream.

Then the river winds through some incised meanders and small lakes and flows off under the bridge that takes the by-road to the village of Leeds. The village is naturally overshadowed by the castle, but St Nicholas' Church is prominent with its massive Norman tower, and a very wide clean interior. A quarter mile away are the extensive but forlorn remains of Leeds Priory with its millpond surrounded by trees. Every time I see abbey and priory ruins I reflect on the politics of envy that led to the decay of many fine buildings in England and throughout Europe as well.

On the other side of the Len, northwards a little stream called the Snagbrook leads to Hollingbourne, itself Saxon—the bourne (stream) of Hola's people—but the area is much older: Roman and Belgic pottery and coins have been found, and somewhere must lie a Roman villa. The village and parish were the homes of a powerful branch of the Culpepers (the church guide disputes the fact of them being the "leading" family, but I think there is little doubt that they had the most influence!) This recalls wife No 5 of Henry VIII, Catherine Howard, the twenty-year-old unfortunate beauty, accused of past indiscretions and adultery with her youthful kinsman, Thomas Culpeper. Full of history I hied to Greenaway Court, forgetting that it was not the original Culpeper home where Catherine lived, and disappointed by its curiously unattractive atmosphere I returned to Hollingbourne. Here was further dismay for the grounds of Hollingbourne Manor, the sixteenth-century Culpeper home, were being "developed"—another strange planning decision and definitely not wanted, so I was told, by many local people.

So to the church which is full of Culpeper memorials; in their chapel the best is the white marble effigy of Lady Elizabeth, but the real glory of the Culpepers here is not stone but needlework. This is kept locked up, but was shown to me by the rector, the Rev. Adrian Bell; they are beautifully embroidered altar and pulpit covers, surrounded by legend and reputed to have been made by the Culpeper daughters whilst their father (Sir John, later Lord) was in exile with the future Charles II. But the great event in the life of Hollingbourne was the earthquake of May 1382 which severely damaged the church; contemporary accounts show a large amount of ragstone ordered from the Maidstone quarries for repair (in Canterbury the cathedral bell tower was destroyed).

Leaving the village I followed the Snagbrook which is a splendid little stream lined with ponds, waterfalls, delightful flower gardens, browsing cattle, geese and tree-lined banks before it burrows under the railway and into a large millpond at Eythorne Street and into the Len once more. In the terraces of the Len along here were found Neolithic and later Bronze Age flints, and after what we saw at Runham there is no doubt that this area has been lived in for many thousands of years, and there must be much more to discover even yet.

At Fulling Mill Farm the Len runs through a gorge; the mill of course has gone but the name recalls the connection with Boxley and fuller's earth to cleanse or "full" the woollen cloth which was often brought from other Wealden streams which had run dry, when by contrast the Len and Loose were flowing freely.

The river now flows through a deep, almost incised valley, and past Milgate where the local limestone outcrops and under a side road, northwards to Bearsted, southwards to Otham. Bearsted is now completely overwhelmed by building, but still retains its fine village green, redolent of the memories of Frank Woolley, perhaps Kent's greatest cricketer who used to play there after his retirement from the county— he was fifty-one when he played his last game for Kent in 1938.

Otham is still a village and has two jewels: Stoneacre, now owned by the National Trust, a fifteenth-century yeoman's house, where you will see the typical "hall" at its best, and along the Langley road the lesser known "Town Hall" built 1480, and added to in 1663. This is a fine large building which you can only peep at for it is very private. Back to the Len and past Gore Court, an old large estate of many owners and uses (but it keeps Otham still green), and then by a wooded side road is Otham church, yet another separated village church on account of the Black Death. This is one of the most attractive places in the entire area, and the old shingled spire fits very well on top of the twelfth-century tower. By the lych-gate are two mounting blocks on either side of the churchyard wall: the inner, for ladies mounting side-saddle, and the outer, the standard type for gentlemen. A local farmer's wife showed me what, it seems, is a recent discovery: a Norman door that may have a passage leading to Willington caves northwards in the local limestone. Inside are some stone brackets and two great nails on a beam which I wondered about; then I learnt that statues stood on the brackets and a large crucifix hung on the nails—all removed presumably in the Reformation. The altar is where it should be, up against the East window, and there is a Latin memorial to Lewin Buff-kyn, 1619, of Gore Court.

This country church may soon be engulfed by the rising tide of suburban building; this has swept along Willington Street northwards from here and urbanized the area with detached boxes of hideous aspect. One pleasant exception is on the sloping street itself where there are some tasteful new terraced houses nicely dove-tailed at different levels, but there are all too few and soon neighbouring Mote Park will be encircled by urban sprawl.

Mote Park, through which the Len flows with a large lake, derives its name doubtless from the Saxon word for meeting place. It is now of environmental value beyond price, and has a long history beginning with weekly markets and annual fairs before becoming a landscaped park in the eighteenth century. It now has returned to its use as a meeting place for county cricket and agricultural shows, as well as being a vast green lung with woods.

At the western end the Len passes through the Turkey Mill, a famous early industrial site where for two centuries fine paper has been made. The paper mill was born in 1719 out of the decay of the cloth industry, as here two converted fulling mills used their old cloth hammers for pounding paper. Water was not only important for power, but as a raw material for brown paper, and white paper used nearby springs. The other raw material, rags, came from the very source of the future market—London—but since Maidstone was a port old ropes and sails could be used for brown paper as on the local Medway mills. The mill got its reputation later by producing fine outsize drawing paper, the enterprise of James Whatman, who utilized another advantage of the river which is shared with the Loose as well. Both have deeply incised valleys and this canalizes the air flow, so that winds can dry the paper hung in drying lofts across the stream.

And so the little river reaches the heart of Maidstone, although partly underground where it reappears and flows in cascades near its old bridge, but rather overwhelmed by the incessant traffic of the inner ring along Mill Street, and at length by the Old Palace Gardens disappears into the Medway.

Part III

THE TIDAL RIVER

11

Chalk and Industry—Maidstone to Rochester

A pleasant way to leave Maidstone for Rochester is to walk through the town by the Medway towpath to Allington Lock. This is surprisingly rural with green expanses of fields and woods near the railway cutting and line to Strood. If you arrive thirsty after your two-mile walk there is the Malta Inn, an old hostelry, now rebuilt into a riverside roadhouse, but still a good place to quench your thirst. Allington Lock, first built in 1792 but now equipped with modern electric sluices, is the meeting point of tidal and upriver waters; the difference between the two is very marked as the tidal water is very foul. On the left bank is a good-looking Victorian lock house and through the surrounding woods can be seen distant Allington Castle. Allington's name is probably derived from a Saxon personal one—Aella's *tun* or dwelling in an enclosure of Aella's people—but this area on a meander of the Medway is prehistoric and was utilized for a Bronze Age village. Later there was a defensive earthwork used by the last Belgae settlers in the valley before the Romans came, yet one more reminder of the age-old settling of this river valley.

The Romans quarried Kentish rag here and transported the stone to London for the city walls. A link with this was discovered in 1962 at Blackfriars in London when a third second-century Roman ship was discovered with a cargo of ragstone in her bottom, pointing to a busy waterborne trade from the Medway. That the settlement was of some importance was hinted at when the site of a villa was unearthed in 1844 south-west of the present Allington Castle.

The later Saxon occupation seems to have been intermittent, very likely on account of the marauding Danes who could easily come upstream this far, with their longboats and great square sails, and making off downstream by turning into the wind and using their oars. Things quietened down later for just before the Norman Conquest King Harold's brother Ulnoth held the manor here.

And so to Allington Castle—the Elentun of Domesday—which is one of those interesting renovated buildings that really need an archaeologist or historian to explain things. The Normans seemed to have built the first castle here for although it was destroyed by royal command (Henry II), the foundations of a massive stone keep with fireplaces and walls have been unearthed. But the castle seen today is the result of three men: Penchester, Wyatt and Conway. Sir Stephen de Penchester (of Penshurst fame) in 1282 built largely what we now see when confronted by the massive gatehouse, faced with Caen stone. The supply of this excellent free-stone from Normandy for this purpose indicates Penchester's position as the King's official, for he was Warden of the Cinque Ports and Constable of Dover Castle. In fact, he started the castle by crenellating a small manor he had built, with towers, a curtain wall and a moat. Allington thus became one of the seven chief or royal castles in Kent.

In 1492 a Yorkshireman, Sir Henry Wyatt, became the owner, but as a loyal follower of the future Henry VII, he fell foul of Richard III, was clapped into the Tower of London and survived through a cat who used to leave pigeons on the ledge of his cell—later cooked by a kindly warder. Not surprisingly cats became the Wyatt mascot. Sir Henry civilized and extended the castle with a long gallery and a Tudor house. Later his more famous poet son, Sir Thomas Wyatt, brought back brown pigeons from Italy in 1526 and they have been bred at Allington ever since; now highly appropriate as the Carmelites who are here have brown habits. Sir Thomas, like Thomas Culpeper, was mixed up with one of Henry VIII's wives, No 2, Anne Boleyn, but unlike Thomas Culpeper he managed to survive. His son in turn, another Sir Thomas, a brave soldier but whose political sense was not equal to his bravery, took part in the abortive Kent rebellion of 1554 against Queen Mary's marriage to Philip of Spain. He completely underestimated popular support; the revolt was an utter failure, and he paid the supreme penalty.

After this the castle slid into a long decline through neglect, became a farm which decayed, and the place was up for sale in 1895 for demolition, but the locals protested and a retired barrister, Falk, rented part of it and grew roses all over the ragstone walls. Then in 1905 Sir Martin Conway, M.P. (later Lord Conway), professor, mountaineer (the boy who climbed the Toad Rock at Tunbridge Wells), entrepreneur and journalist, along with his American wife bought, saved and restored the castle, living in it until 1932. The family sold it in 1951 to the Carmelites from the Aylesford Friars, and later in 1972 it became an independent Priory of the Carmelite community who have kept it in good repair and are actively continuing restoration. An ironic fact when one considers that Allington in Tudor times was a centre of the Reformation!

From Allington perhaps it is appropriate to go to Boxley on the flanks of the chalk downs where there was an early Cistercian abbey (1146), the only one in Kent; and now all that is left is a great tithe barn. I am afraid that for once the abbey's dissolution was probably deserved as it had a frightful reputation for fraudulent acts by the monks. The village is still pleasant and I found All Saints' Church so clean and polished that I felt like removing my shoes. The most interesting monuments are to Sir Henry Wyatt "fed and preserved by a cat". The other is of Tennyson's sister. It is thought that the Boxley Brook that runs into the Medway was the original of his poem; its surroundings are rather different now. Up at the top of the hill near a very handsome pumping station (built in 1939) is Boxley House, the remains of a manor given by Henry VIII along with the abbey to the Wyatts. Today it is a country club and its chief claim to fame is literary, in that it appears as Lord Hornblower's residence from 1820 in Parkinson's book about the admiral. Although the area is still rural, it is encircled by a twentieth-century evil, traffic noise, for not far away is the M20, and the A229 Chatham road is a motorway in noise if not in name.

This insistent drone disturbed me as I searched for Cobtree Manor at nearby Sandling, reputed to be the original of Dingley Dell in *The Pickwick Papers*. Pickwick's famous soliloquy when he opened his lattice window and " . . . the rich, sweet smell of the hayricks rose to his chamber window" was at Dingley Dell. It is extraordinary that in 1924 a writer said that in no way does the prospect around Cobtree belie the description of Manor Farm at Dingley Dell. But alas, all that is now a memory.

The river approach to Aylesford is distinctly more pleasant than that by road, for we are now getting near to the industrialized river. The approach by road is dominated by the Forstal Industrial Estate. These ill-named excrescences that swallow up so much open land as though modern man, like Nature, abhors a vacuum are neither industrial nor estates, often being merely commercial plots of vast boxlike uninteresting warehouses. There is no actual industry.

The sight from the bank upstream of the village, church and Medway bridge is idyllic. The name Eles-fort, or Aeglesford, indicates an ancient crossing place at low tide but its meaning is not very clear. Aylesford is one of the oldest inhabited sites in

England but inevitably some of the history is more legendary than actual. Much more is known about its prehistoric Belgic and Roman past than the shadowy period that followed. Hengist, Horsa, and Vortigern may well be legendary figures, in spite of the *Anglo-Saxon Chronicle*. However, Aylesford's history is more substantial concerning the depredations of the Danes, for in 1016 King Edmund, after beating the Danes at Otford and driving them into the Medway and on to Sheppey, then met the local Kentish chiefs at Aylesford and rather unwisely decided not to follow up their victory.

The village high street, which I used to know very well, profoundly disappointed me on my last visit. It had an air of hollowness and disuse. I suppose years of heavy traffic and encroaching industrial development seemed to have got the better of it, finalized by the closing of the "George" pub. It was almost a relief to climb up to St Peter's Church on its hill. The dominating tower, which like so many in Kent is mainly fifteenth century, has its lower part Norman with Roman tiles—a realistic reminder of local history. Inside are two enormous memorials, a Culpeper (Sir Thomas, 1604) once more, this time from the family that lived over the river at the earlier Preston Manor for four hundred years. The later Victorian Preston Hall is now the core of the famous British Legion Village.

The other vast monument is to the Banks family, all in semi-Roman costume. The interest here is that Sir John was an early "hop baron" and his farm accounts have survived. He had 20 or 30 acres of hops in Aylesford and in 1679 they cost him nearly £300—three items were about the same: dressing (including weeding), hop poles, and picking. This was just before one of the worst climatic shocks in British history—the 1690s; in 1695 there were no hops at all, and in 1696 they were worth next to nothing.

Further downstream, along the·river on the bank amid trees with an old ragstone river wall, are the carefully restored buildings of the Friars, the first English Carmelite foundation of 1242. Like many buildings of this kind, it has had a long history of troubled affairs, and the Order was dissolved in 1538 when the zealous Reformationist, Sir Thomas Wyatt, received it and promptly destroyed some of the buildings for their lead roofing. In 1675 it belonged to the Banks family, the "hop barons", and they at least renovated it with new windows. Finally in 1930 the main block was burnt down. After 700 years the Carmelites returned and in 1951 the Friary was rededicated. It is now a beautiful group of buildings which is seen especially well from the opposite bank.

Beyond here at Millhall are the wharves of one of the outports of Maidstone. From here went fuller's earth from Boxley— apparently nearly all to the East Coast (though some went illegally elsewhere!)—and most of the Kentish iron and some from Sussex. Here too was where John Browne kept his teams of oxen, so important for hauling the cannon through the Wealden mud.

From now on the real industrialization of the lower Medway begins; although not very pretty it has been an important part of north Kent's economy for well over a century. Dominating everything here are the huge Reed paper mills at New Hythe. The actual paper-making process is a vast exercise and the mill here specializes in newsprint, packaging papers, and the conversion of what is called base paper (recycled waste paper) into high-grade printing and special copying paper. An interesting process that Reed pioneered is the de-inking of waste paper; 95 per cent of a newspaper has never had ink on it and if you can get rid of the ink of course the paper can be used again and again.

The location of these works was on reclaimed land taking advantage of good communications by river and railway. The Medway water is not used for paper-making but for cooling purposes and water for the paper-making process is taken from bore holes at the site. Nowadays of course roads are important but the railway still brings in oil for boiler fuel. Originally the local labour force was not really suitable for modern paper-making and Scottish paper-makers had to be brought in, but during the slump Reed's did provide good employment for local skilled people such as electricians and other specialists, and now many local people are employed as workmen, apprentices, engineers and in management. The diversity of products has been a necessary part of paper-making history along the Medway. One interesting sideline here is a plant on the Reed site which separates wheat flour into gluten and starch, the latter going to the papermills and the gluten going into "slimmers' rolls" and sold to bakers.

It is a fascinating experience to see paper being made, especially watching the water being removed from the moving mesh. And in spite of strong Canadian and Scandinavian competition and the necessity for continual improvements in very expensive plant and machinery Reed's do their best to observe strict environmental regulations, like recycled water, which if it cannot be recycled within the production process it is totally refined before being returned to one of the local rivers.

Now is the place to look upwards at the chalk downs and realize that this whole lower Medway area is rich in prehistoric remains. Westwards from the vast gravel lakes between New Hythe and Snodland, near the prehistoric track called the Pilgrims' Way, is the long barrow of Coldrum. This is a 4,000-year-old stone burial chamber above Ryarsh Wood with a fine view of the valley, and worth the walk to it. It is the best Neolithic monument in either Kent or Surrey.

Less than a mile away (1 kilometre) is Trottiscliffe (pronounced Trosley) church, a most interesting early Norman, plain little building with a high pulpit and box pews. Some of the Neolithic remains from Coldrum are kept here in a case on the north wall, and the west wall is a remarkable example of modern flintwork (1885). The flints are varied: local black from Wrotham, red from Halling, the cross from Norfolk and most of the rest from the chalk pit at Greenhythe. There was a church orchestra at one time, and I noticed a tambourine hanging on the wall which was presented by Miss Shrubsole, whose father Albert aged ten had played it in 1897.

The village has some good houses, including the weatherboarded one in which the painter Graham Sutherland lived, but I found it has become rather suburban, and even noisy—hardly surprising with the M20, A20 and A25 complex just below.

From the downland slopes we return to industry at Snodland, an unlovely place but notable for a prehistoric crossing place to Burham over the river, Roman remains and an Anglo-Saxon cemetery. It is here that the second important industry along the river really begins—cement. The material of course is old— the Romans made a variety that has never yielded its secret— and in the eighteenth century there were many experiments of clay and lime to make a cement or hydraulic mortar. The modern "Portland Cement" was invented by Joseph Aspdin in 1824 who thought that when it was spread on a wall it looked like Portland limestone. He little imagined that his product would lead to deep chalk pits, scarred hillsides, tall chimneys, belching smoke and a grey dust spreading over all. Here at Snodland the raw materials were readily at hand—chalk and Medway mud, dried, burnt to fusion point and then ground to a fine powder. William Lee's original works here were sold to the British Portland Cement Company in 1839.

We cross the river again at Aylesford by the medieval bridge, originally of eight arches, but reduced to five in the last century for the needs of navigation, to continue the prehistoric trail to Kit's Coty—a favourite picnic spot of Charles Dickens, by the way, where he insisted that all his guests cleared up all the litter. This is on a natural bench of the chalk slopes and the most famous of the Neolithic chambered tombs. The burial chamber is built of sarsen stones, rather curious sandstone boulders which were common on the chalk from the time when in the Eocene geological period (about 50 million years ago) sandy lagoons lay on part of the chalk surface. The original barrow or mound was denuded by ploughing. There are other sarsens scattered around, some with fanciful names like Countless Stones, White Horse, and Little Kit's Coty, which are all remains of a great necropolis either destroyed by eighteenth-century ploughing or even nineteenth-century gunpowder. These Medway tombs are closely related to similar ones in North Germany and the Netherlands, and suggest the long connection that this river region has had with the North Sea lands.

This fertile area also attracted the Romans and not far off were sited clusters of their villas. The most recent discovery was at Eccles, near Aylesford, in 1962 which was a large commercial Romano-British villa farm with bath houses and possibly a tile kiln and a pottery which covered a period from not long after the famous Medway battle up to the fourth century. The whole site seems to have been on a palatial scale from the outset with a military style of planning, precise dating of which is not yet complete. It is now covered with a barley field, but the local farmer, Mr Midge, who is extremely interested and knowledgeable about archaeology, told me some curious tales about this site. He has found many Roman tiles and great lumps of ragstone in his fields—traces of a Roman wall. In one field, which apparently has throughout the centuries always been pasture, there is a curious straight furrowed ridge which his horses have always shied at in the evening light; it is said that over the years many skeletons have been found in the vicinity. And Mr Midge has a Morello cherry tree which died this year and was the favourite "rubbing tree" of his old grey mare Donna who had died the previous year aged twenty-six.

Eccles of course is old; the name is from Eclesia, late Latin for church, derived through Aiglessa, which means the site could have been a Roman Christian one (like its sister village Eccles Street in Norfolk). The present village is nineteenth-century industrial in form from the cement industry, whose abandoned clay pit near the river is now filled with water and called Eccles Lake. This lake stores pumped water taken from the Medway at Springfield (Maidstone) before going to the Burham Treatment Works and passed into the public supply.

Burham itself is rather a dull village in pleasant open chalk country, below which near the river bank is a more interesting rather untidy place called Burham Court. St. Mary's Church here is one of those unfortunate old buildings which have become redundant. But I obtained a large bunch of keys and went inside via three padlocks plus one more to climb the bell tower. The church is bare, but there were two things of interest: one an enormous bell cast in 1300 which I believe may well be the oldest in England, and the other a wooden brass-banded barrel labelled "one Lord, one Faith, one Baptism". From the top of the bell tower, although it was a very cold grey April morning, the view of the great meander called Horseshoe Reach was superb, backed by the paper and cement complex at Snodland.

Further along near the waterfront was the site of a Roman building, whose use puzzled archaeologists but is now thought to be a vault for the wine trade. As there were also remnants of a wharf it seems one more piece of evidence that the Roman Medway was a flourishing commercial waterway. Some of the waterfront here is of a minor messy industrial nature, but in the evening sunshine of late September all this faded away for I caught the scent of waterside flowers. The tide was high and after a small launch chugged past, two swans drifted slowly downstream by the reed-fringed Holborough Marshes and all looked and felt tranquil. Industry, marshes, chalk and the muddy river sometimes combine here to make pottering about very enjoyable.

At this point you realize that the Medway is entering its great Chalk Gap, cut a few million years before the Ice Ages when the river was flowing at about the chalk level following the retreat of the Calabrian Sea that had lapped the shores of the Wealden island in a landscape utterly different from today.

This lower part of the Medway is ideal for showing the typical brackish tidal vegetation which you can see when following the path from Burham Court round the meander opposite industrial Snodland. On the inner part of the meander in the flood plain the river leaves a generous amount of fine silt on which grows a reed swamp. This is our tallest native grass—it can reach 11 feet (3.4 metres)—and the leafy canes have purple-brown plumes in the summer changing to bare brown stems in the winter. Behind this on the drier ground is the marsh pasture with the pink of marsh-mallow and golden dock flowers giving plenty of colour. Over the years the outer part of the meander has had its banks stabilized by stone walls and so the land is free from tidal waters and then a good drained pasture is often made. Behind this, waterside trees and shrubs of alder, ash and even oak often develop, as you can see downstream on both banks.

Burham Court to Wouldham is a pleasant little jaunt on foot, but Wouldham village has, it seems, turned its back on the river and development has been limited to new houses. Some of these indeed are quite good-looking with dormers, pleasant windows with glazing bars and nice little doorways. The thirteenth-century church with its fifteenth-century post-Black Death tower (as I explained in Chapter IX) has one of the most poignant memories of Trafalgar in the grave of Walter Burke, the *Victory*'s purser, whose arms supported the dying Nelson.

Beyond Wouldham I went to see Starkey Castle, a reputedly fifteenth-century manor house obviously much altered and now a farmhouse. I was quite unable to decide whether it was being restored or being returned to ruin.

Prominently now on the skyline is the great cantilever motorway bridge across the river, a fine piece of pioneer engineering, for when it was built it was the largest bridge of pre-stressed concrete. It is 3,272 feet long (almost a kilometre) with a 500-foot (150 metre) central span, and it is possible to walk across the bridge and thus get to Cuxton and Halling. Not that you might want to stop long there as they are old industrial areas expanded and worsened by vast new housing at Cuxton and the eternal traffic. Old industry—which I find far less intrusive—you can escape, new housing sometimes, but the wretched traffic never.

However, up above all this on the wooded and, in places, scarred chalk slopes narrow roads and lanes lead to wide prospects and at length to Cobham. This pleasant village has three things worth seeing, not in order of worthiness but convenience. Firstly, Cobham College, the sixteenth-century almshouses, originally Sir John de Cobham's fourteenth-century chantry, a place of worship endowed for chanting masses for the souls of the departed. Next, the Leather Bottle Inn, of *Pickwick* fame, but damaged exactly 100 years ago by fire, so some of the timber is modern, nevertheless the inn is still redolent of Mr Tupman. Thirdly, and best of all, at the other end of the village is the modest Caroline house (1683-4) built of locally fired small red bricks with wide lime mortar joints (also local) called "Owletts" and put up for Farmer Hayes and his wife who seemed to have been typical prosperous Restoration cherry, hop and corn growers. I saw it in the late afternoon and was shown over by the son of the man whose personality the house reflects: Sir Herbert Baker, the British Empire architect, whose family acquired "Owletts" in the nineteenth century through marriage. What you see here is a splendid staircase—opulent for such a small house—above which is a superb original plaster ceiling, and for me quite the best small dining-room I have ever seen. It is dominated by a large Elizabethan refectory table, taken from the old kitchen, a magnificent article for which Sir Herbert made a new top in 1920, and after sixty years of scrubbing only with wood ash is the same colour as the original. The walls here now reveal the original yellow pine and the upper panels of cedarwood which were added later. In the living-room full of interesting objects is the famous Empire Clock installed in 1933, which shows the time in various parts of the old British Empire. The garden, once a farmyard, has an octagonal sunken-garden built over the old duckpond; this design harmonizes with the octagonal bay extension from the library. All these alterations are tasteful and well executed—as only a good architect would undertake.

North-east of the village, standing in magnificent parkland now with its wooded border along the M2 is Cobham Hall, once the Tudor mansion of the 10th Lord Cobham who rebuilt it—if that is the word—from an old, rather modest manor house. From 1584 to 1602 he built two enormous wings outwards from the ends of the old house with octagonal lead-capped turrets at each end of these wings. He didn't use only bricks, but got permission from Henry IV of France (Henri de Navarre) to import 200 tons (!) of Caen stone which he used for the porch.

After this the Cobhams fell into disgrace, for the son, Henry Brooke, the 11th Lord, forfeited the estate by trying to put a Stuart lady on the throne in place of James VI of Scotland. Among the long list of happenings and owners that followed three are worth a mention. The first is Frances, Duchess of Lennox, the chatelaine for ten Restoration years and known as "La Belle Stuart" (much admired by Charles II) who was the original of Britannia on our coins and also responsible for the blue and gold of naval officers' uniforms—they were the colours and design of her riding habit.

Next, in 1790, is Humphrey Repton who redesigned the gardens and landscaped the park, the legacy of which is a thousand-yard-long avenue of lime trees and two thousand laburnums planted in the pleasure grounds. And with this came the Bligh family, Earls of Darnley, who did so much for cricket in Cobham, Kent and England from 1776 to 1882. They pioneered early matches, founded the village club, played for Kent, and finally brought back the Ashes from Australia. Cobham Hall is now a girls' school, but can be visited at certain times.

From here one ought to visit two places to see the fantastic contrast between the rural and industrial Kent of the Medway region. Down some side roads and under the old Chatham main line after about 2 miles (3 kilometres) you will come to the tiny hamlet of Luddesdown which has a church, a pub, a few houses and Luddesdown Court, a house that has been lived in for over 900 years since Bishop Odo of Bayeux (mentioned in Chapter VI) inhabited it.

Four miles from here (7 kilometres) lies Strood. I will spare you the town but not the squalor of its waterfront which I happened on whilst trying to find the Temple Manor, one of its more interesting buildings. In the foreshore mud off Strood Yacht Club I saw the following: a wheelbarrow, supermarket trolley, wooden reel of stout wire cable, netting, two gangways, rotting timbers, complete sink unit, wire tray and wooden mooring platforms with ring-bolts. Kent has often been called the Garden of England; not long ago a friend of mine referred to the Medway Towns as "the compost heap". In the next chapter we shall try to disprove that statement, hopefully!

12

The Medway Towns

Strood, Rochester, Chatham, Gillingham and Rainham today form a vast conurbation of nearly 300,000 people which sweeps across the Medway and its estuary shores. For nearly 200 years the first three have almost been indistinguishable from each other. When he saw them in 1724 Daniel Defoe said: "Rochester, Stroud and Chatham are three distinct places but contiguous except the interval of the river between the two first and a very small marsh or vacancy between Rochester and Chatham."

It is on this subject that we meet our first Dickensian character called Richard Doubledick from the "Seven Poor Travellers", who in 1799 tramped, as he said, "into Rochester or Chatham because if anybody knows to a nicety where Rochester ends and Chatham begins it is more than I do". For many years three separate boroughs existed with Strood as a poor relation, being a rural district council. Even now Gillingham and Rainham are separate from the new Borough of Medway. But in spite of these separate identities, for many centuries the most important town, or even the only town, was Rochester. And in the early eighteenth century even this town hadn't a great reputation, for as Defoe said: "There is little remarkable in Rochester, except the ruins of a very old castle, and an antient but not extraordinary cathedral . . ."

The name of the first Celtic settlement made by the Belgae was called Durobrivae at about 100 B.C., and was adopted by the Romans for their later important capital of one of their *civitates*, or civil districts. This was a walled city of 23 acres (10 hectares) and its remains are still being unearthed, as in Minor Canon Row recently; walls make good history books for on the waterfront Esplanade is a wall showing three Roman courses, some Norman walling and thirteenth-century repair work. Thus Rochester's history is really rooted in the Roman period, because in the confused era that followed the departure of the Roman military presence Britain was still a Roman island if not a Roman province. Even as late as 455 the British Church still had contact with Rome.

The Saxons renamed the town Rofesceastre which was recognition that the town's origin was Roman. In 604 the long-submerged memory of Christianity because a reality with the establishment of a bishopric by Justus, but in 676 Rochester and its church were destroyed by Ethelred, King of the Mercians, and its bishop, Putta, driven into exile, making no attempt to recover his see. However, in spite of these setbacks there is a hint of continuity of life in Rochester for a Saxon coin minted in the ninth century perpetuates the old Roman name as "Doro-brebia". Certainly in 886 the town walls were strong enough to be besieged and keep the Danes at bay until King Alfred and his army arrived to rescue the city.

Rochester, like Tonbridge, was an ancient river crossing point, and its history—as with its later neighbours—can be traced through its communications. The tidal Medway was a point of entry into south-east England from ancient times, and even the Phoenician traders may have come upriver to Alling-ton. The Romans were much greater users of the river than has been recorded; they used wharves rather than an actual port, and probably much of their trade was carried on with the help of units of the Classis Britannica (provincial flotilla) based at Richborough in its supply role. The Saxon penetration of the Medway area was more often by small groups of farmers than by large forces. But the Danes knew how to use the river; they plundered Rochester, and after the attack in 886 King Alfred sent a "naval" force into East Anglia from here, which might be said to mark the birth of the Royal Navy in the Medway.

The Normans decided the best defence of this vital crossing point was a castle, and typical of their engineering skill, Bishop Gundulf—a great architect—built a tower bailey in 1087. Later in 1127 a superb keep was added which is what we see today, and the castle had many uses; one was as a top-security prison, when the wife of the Scottish King Bruce was held here.

However, the port of Rochester really grew up by the stimulus of its entrepôt trade with Maidstone and the wharves down-stream at Millhall and New Hythe. This flourished from medieval times and expanded mightily with Tudor iron, and later the paper industry, always being swelled with the tra-ditional products of Kent like fruit and hops, especially cherries, all brought down by barge or the small sailing craft known as hoys. Kent was no great dairy county, and there was a brisk coastal trade with East Anglia which sent butter and cheese, and more and more coal came from Newcastle and Sunderland. The other great local commerce was in fuller's earth from Boxley which went in huge quantities to Colchester for the East Anglian cloth areas, and a fair amount went illegally to Holland at high prices—the port paid for this in another way for it was prosecuted in the 1630s in the Star Chamber. Holland was the main importer of Rochester's oysters, and in return sent cheese, bricks and tiles (the Dutch were already masters at making these with many beautiful patterns).

Nevertheless, Rochester's trade was more and more drawn into the maw of another great entrepôt—London—and would be so until roads got better. Rochester's ships were often owned by large groups of people, and one, the *Blessing* of 1637, was in shares as small as one-sixteenth, held mainly by Maidstone folk. Once Chatham Dockyard rose to importance Rochester began to import softwood from the Baltic, which continued into the nineteenth century when one of the better smells in the Medway was the scent of pinewood from Scandinavia. This century was the heyday of sail, and an incredible variety of craft would be seen in the river: small topsail schooners, dumpy collier brigs, graceful Scandinavian barques, upriver "stumpy" barges and the most familiar and characteristic of all—the spritsail and topsail barges. The later lasted well into our own time, and in 1964 I remember when I was a Merchant Service Officer outward bound in the Thames estuary seeing an Everard sailing barge (the last working one) making its way downriver with its tan sails.

Rochester today is an efficient small port with a thriving coastal trade to Europe, still handling timber and bulk cargoes like granite, sand, ballast, cement, forest products, as well as perishables like fruit and vegetables. For me, Blue Boar Pier, Limehouse and Stanley Wharves are as much Rochester as the castle and cathedral.

But down on the waterfront we are almost in Chatham which began life as a small village on a wooded peninsula. An earlier name was Ceteham—a personal name, Cete's "ham", or homestead, in the forest. This village was insignificant until Henry VIII realized the value of the anchorage when England's first great warship *Henri Grace à Dieu* or *Great Harry* was built here in 1512, with four masts and (much later in 1540) its guns arranged in two tiers. The tidal flats were convenient for heeling a ship over so that it could be "graved", or have its weed-encrusted hull scraped or burned before being tarred. The first actual yards were laid down in Elizabeth's reign before the Armada, and dockyard officials lived in Tudor houses—now well known to visitors—Satis and Eastgate, which are of course in Rochester.

The dockyard as we know it now was begun in 1618 in James I's reign, but by 1665 its reputation had declined when Pepys visited it to see Commissioner Pett; as he put it, it was a case of "four horses drawing a piece of wood that a man could carry". Overmanning and corruption hinted at the disasters to come with the Dutch raids two years later. But dockyard activity by the end of the seventeenth century meant that Chatham with 5,000 people was larger than Rochester, and Chatham's naval supremacy continued with the salt marshes of St Mary's Island being made into dock basins.

Dickens's picturesque fictional characters, so beloved of modern Medway tourism, tend to overshadow Dickens's less affectionate memories of the Navy—he was after all from a dockyard family—and in 1851 he wrote: "More obstruction of good things and patronage of bad things, more extravagances, jobbery, ignorance, conceit, saving of cheeseparings, and waste of gold have been committed in these dockyards (as in everything connected with the misdirection of the Navy) than in every branch of the public service put together."

Parkinson provides a better picture of the nineteenth-century navy with his Hornblower biography, when as a full admiral Hornblower is C-in-C at Chatham, and becomes interested in steam propulsion in 1835-8. Steam power of course eventually led to a vast increase in the size of warships and Chatham became less important because the large battleships and battle cruisers could not get into the dockyard. But the fact of proximity to London also meant in two world wars proximity to the enemy. In November 1914, early in the First World War, the 15,000-ton battleship H.M.S. *Bulwark* blew up whilst loading ammunition with the loss of 800 sailors, and in September 1917 came a foretaste of a future war. There was an air raid on Chatham by Gotha bombers, where a relatively small bomb (110 pounds) caused more casualties than anything else dropped in the entire war when it fell on Chatham barracks and killed 136 naval ratings.

In the Second World War Chatham was very much a base for smaller craft, particularly submarines. My first experiences of Medway mud were when I was serving in H.M. Submarine *Sirdar* and we acted as a "guinea pig" for the German adaptation of a Dutch invention called the Snorkel, which allowed a submerged submarine to charge her batteries. This was done by a portable flap valve which let air in whilst the diesels were running and automatically closed if the pipe went below the surface. This was a very painful process for our eardrums as the air pressure in the boat varied so much. For some weeks the Medway was not our favourite part of Kent for we were in it too much without seeing it!

The submarine tradition continues with the refitting and refuelling of nuclear-powered boats, and some have been built in the dockyard. Although the Navy has become part of an international force, "Tiddley Chats" is still important as a naval base despite, sadly, the Royal Marines being no longer there.

The Medway was not only a highway and anchorage, but valuable for fishing, although the estuary was not generally esteemed for ordinary, or what was called "floating fish". But it was important for its oyster beds, a local industry for hundreds of years with a London home market, and a Dutch export market. It was controlled by an Admiralty Court from Rochester; this was granted in 1446 by Henry VI to the Admiral of the Medway, who is the Mayor. This picturesque court still sits once a year on a barge moored to Rochester Pier, to decide on matters of apprenticeship to the oyster traders and free fishermen—although the state of the river and its busy shipping precludes oysters these days. One sunny Sunday morning in April I talked to an old fisherman down in the port at Rochester, and he told me that you could still catch codling and eels—mainly on a flooding tide, but sometimes on an ebbing one. Fishing was poor with high tides, as the river was so dirty, but in any case the whole thing was very variable indeed—as I suppose it always has been.

The Mayor—nowadays of Rochester-upon-Medway after having been called Medway for a few years—still beats his bounds from the Hawkwood Stone (the Maidstone boundary) to Garrison Point off Sheerness. This interesting ceremony is carried out with the co-operation of the Rochester Cruising Club and escorted by all manner of craft belonging to the Medway Port Authority, Royal Engineers, Southern Water, Trinity House, Police and perhaps best of all by an old bawley boat (local fishing craft) built a century ago.

Through the kindness of a former mayor and a local businessman with Belgian connections I was lucky enough to go on this cruise in 1980, which that particular year revived the old custom of the Lord Mayor of London visiting the London Stone at Lower Upnor marking the boundary of the fishing rights of the

City of London. This started when Richard the Lion-heart found wars and crusades expensive nearly 800 years ago. He got his money by granting an obscure charter to the Lord Mayor of London giving him powers of jurisdiction "over the river of Thames and waters of Medway". The seaward limits were always vague, and there were many disputes over fishing with the Men of Kent, as can be imagined. Unfortunately, the day in July I went on this interesting voyage the weather was filthy and in keeping with an awful wet month, so it was seen through high wind and sweeping rainstorms, which made me think that if the weather had been like that in the past the fishermen would have been left in peace!

Ever since the Romans built their road from Southwark to Dover, the Via Strata or Watling Street or nowadays the A2, which was their most important road and ours too for many centuries, the river crossing at Rochester was a problem. It is wide and deep with very strong tidal currents.

The Belgae destroyed their own bridge in the Roman campaign of A.D. 43 and the only evidence of the important Roman bridge is a few piles in the river bed. The early medieval bridge was complete with drawbridge and barbican and maintained by an extraordinary communal group consisting of the King, Archbishop of Canterbury, Bishop of Rochester, and local Hundreds and villages, each responsible for odd piers and spans. But baronial revolts and sieges, fireships, iceflows, flood water and would-be arsonists all contributed at length to the building of a stone bridge in 1392 which lasted until 1856. In 1724 Defoe described it as "the largest, highest and strongest built of all the bridges in England, except London Bridge . . ."

In 1857 the Royal Engineers blew up the old bridge in spectacular fashion, but some of the stone has survived to form the fine balustrade along the River Esplanade. The replacement bridge had become necessary because of shoaling and obstruction to navigation by the enormous starlings (projections of piling out from the lower part of the piers) which affected the tidal flow.

The period that followed saw the greatest increase in size of ships since the world began, and less than fifty years after the new bridge had been built the cast-iron arches had to be replaced by flat girders to allow ships to pass underneath. The latest road bridge was adapted in 1970 from the old Chatham railway bridge which ran parallel to the older road bridge. After all the rude remarks that various writers have made about this structure, I for one was rather pleased that in a sense it "got its own back" to help out with the appalling weight of road traffic that now crosses the Medway. This was done through the Bridge Wardens, an ancient bridge-maintenance trust dating from the stone bridge in 1391 and whose present board room was once the bridge chapel (provided by Sir John de Cobham, who had so much to do with building the bridge). After the dissolution the building deteriorated and was restored in our own time by Sir Herbert Baker, the Empire and Kentish architect whose house we saw at Cobham.

The Dover Road enters the conurbation at the dreary town of Strood, which although it doesn't look it, is quite an old place which had a number of hospitals to care for travellers—particularly the Canterbury pilgrims. It is said that they preferred to stay at Strood rather than Rochester because the cathedral monks were annoyed by the pilgrims going on to Canterbury to offer gifts at the shrine of St. Thomas à Becket, as there was no shrine of such stature at Rochester. One thinks nowadays of leprosy as a tropical disease, but in the early Tudor period a lazar house existed at the top of Strood Hill for lepers who had to rely on alms from passing travellers or pilgrims.

From the bridge the Dover Road led to Rochester High Street and was literally the backbone of Dickens's association with the Medway Towns. This area had an extraordinary attraction for him, and provided many novels and stories—without which the city's tourism would apparently collapse. But Rochester High Street is much more than just Dickens, for it is the most historic street that the Medway traveller will see from Ashdown Forest to Sheerness.

Why this is so can only be appreciated by a slow walk with an enquiring eye, because much of the less well-known history is in odd corners and on walls. From the bridge end on the right is a very ordinary building (rebuilt 1864) which was the site of the original Crown Inn from the early fourteenth century, where a whole host of royalty stayed (Anne of Cleves, Queen Mary, Philip of Spain, Elizabeth, and Charles I). In 1758, after walking from Gravesend (!), Hogarth the painter had a typical repast here: soles, flounders with crab sauce, roast stuffed calf's head, fried ham, roast mutton and green peas, small beer and port.

Just past the Crown Inn is the eighteenth-century Royal Victoria and Bull Hotel, used by Dickens factually and fictionally, and opposite is the 1687 Guildhall (now a museum) which has a very fine plaster ceiling. Further on is, to my mind, the best single building in the street: the 1706 Corn Exchange given by Sir Cloudesley Shovell with its attractive projecting clock.

Past the Cathedral precincts on the left is the 1579 Watts Charity, founded by a Tudor dockyard official for six poor travellers to stay overnight. It has been completely refurbished and upstairs is a little galleried Elizabethan bedroom and a very cosy sitting-room. Here on an unpleasant April day I had a chat over a cup of tea with Mr Stevenson, who had been Head Verger and associated with the Cathedral for thirty years. He gave me a very interesting vignette of modern Cathedral city life, where it seems that bureaucracy has invaded the ecclesiastical sphere as cathedrals become more important to a town for tourism than for worship.

The Cathedral I find difficult to describe, although I have been inside for Matins and Evensong and walked all around it. Practically all periods of church architecture exist here side by side, and there is of course the famous Norman west front doorway, which was peeped into by one of Dickens's characters, Mr Grewgious, who said: "Dear me, it's like looking down the throat of Old Time". All old cathedrals give one the feeling of great age, but here in Rochester it seems intensified, probably because the site as a Christian place of worship is so old, for at this western end was the apse of the old Saxon church with its wide nave. The present Norman nave is the best of what is seen of Bishop Gundolf's work inside, as outside his tower is engulfed with its fourteenth-century completion, and the top with its short spire was added in 1904. Next door is the church of St Nicholas built in 1423, which the Rochester people used after a quarrel with the Cathedral monks; it is now Diocesan offices, and opposite is an old Catalpa tree (Red Indian Bean Tree) often described wrongly as rare, for they are quite frequently seen in parks and gardens; the effect of all this in the Cathedral precincts is rather pleasant.

Just off the High Street there is a real gem in the delightful square of La Providence. This was rebuilt from nineteen old terraced houses that formed the 1840s Theobalds Square that was very down-at-heel; it now houses fifty-three flats for the elderly descendants of the French Huguenots who first came to Britain in the sixteenth century. Originally the French Hospital was founded to care for those refugees who were poor and aged, and was finally established in 1718 by George I in a Royal Charter (in which he is described as King of France!) at Bath Street, London. In 1865 they moved to Victoria Park, Hackney

(now ironically a Catholic Convent) where they were undis-
turbed until 1934 when Herbert Morrison's L.C.C. cast envious
eyes on it—for compulsory purchase! War came and afterwards
for a short while they were in Sussex, and finally their fourth
home is here; it was shown to me with great aplomb by the
Steward, Mr Davies. This included the General Court presided
over by an elected Governor—for 200 years from the Pleydell-
Bouverie family (Earls of Radnor)—and the Community's
treasures like the 1632 communion cup, salvers and silver loving cups. It is fitting that they are now in Kent on the Medway for
their ancestors brought the hop to England and improved the
British diet by gardening and vegetable growing. Later they
improved the art of dyeing, and it was their famous Wands-
worth Scarlet that was adopted by the British Army for their
"Red Coats". One family were the de la Rues, the famous specialist paper-makers, but less well known are the Fourdrinier
brothers who developed the paper machine using water pulp
from a French invention by Nicholas Robert (1798) in France
itself, and of course so important in the Medway mills.

We are now abreast of Eastgate House, the 1590 dwelling of
another Tudor dockyard personage, Sir Peter Buck, Paymaster
to the Navy. This became the City Museum in 1903 where
Dickens had a room—now he seems to be the chief resident! Two
of the more interesting exhibits are outside: Dickens's chalet via
Gadshill and Cobham Park and a piece of Roman road—
Watling Street.

No 69, now Lloyd's Bank, was the house of Sir Richard Head,
who sheltered James II of England and VII of Scotland after his
unfortunate experiences at the hands of Faversham "fishermen
and rabble", to quote Defoe (who had fought against James II at
Sedgemoor). Defoe strongly disapproved of their behaviour
against "his majesty . . . with such indignity in his person".

Above ground one is constantly reminded of Dickens, below
ground of Rome, for south of the street in Eagle Court down
Eagle Alley another part of the Roman wall has been revealed
with some medieval work. Further on down into Eastgate there
are the large old gabled buildings (mostly from 1684) which
housed Dickens's Pumblechook and Sapsea, and so we come to
Star Hill where the Roman road to Sussex begins. The actual
road line is along Delce Road, and upwards close to the junction
with the modern A229 Maidstone Road stood the working corn
mill of Delce. This was the sole survivor of twenty-two city mills
and was rather stupidly destroyed in 1947 by a greengrocer. It

was really quite modern being a tall octagonal smock mill rebuilt in 1872 and worked by both wind and steam with a roller plant, and by it was a small jam factory which until the 1930s sold delicious preserves.

Atop Star Hill are the 1805 St Catherine's Hospital alms-houses, long and low with really well-kept gardens fronting this busy main road. The A2 shoots off here as the New Road, an early example (1769) of a by-pass to avoid the frightful conges-tion even then of the "double" High Streets of Rochester-Chatham. Above the grassy slopes here stood Fort Pitt, part of Chatham's nineteenth-century defences, now a girls' school, under which are the railway tunnels and from the top of which is a wide view over the river. I once applied for a job at Fort Pitt School, but was refused on account of being a bachelor, "What—not *even* engaged?" was the surprised remark on learning of my shameful single state.

Modern Chatham is dominated by two buildings: the 1899 Town Hall and the new Pentagon complex, but the best recent addition is the Riverside Gardens developed from the old Naval Gun Wharf, whilst the best old buildings are within the dock-yard including the fine 1720 main gate.

Further along the A2 is Gillingham, which is really Victorian New Brompton, and was the home of many who served in the Navy or worked in the dockyard. It contains Kent's only Foot-ball League team; this has never been really successful and demonstrates the peculiar separateness of the Medway Towns. With their large population they ought to have a first-class side.

By far the most interesting Gillingham inhabitant was long ago, a man called William Adams who in 1600 visited Japan, married a Japanese girl and became worshipped as a Shinto god. Its most interesting building, if a trifle odd, was the curious cubic Jezreel's Tower named from a leader of a religious sect, an ex-soldier called James Jezreel who sponsored immortality and died in 1885. His tower, never completed, was well built of good materials, and defied attempts by the Borough at adaptation, so tiring of this they eventually destroyed it. The latest effort here is the development of the old Gordon Barracks, once the home of the Royal Engineers, into an industrial park. Time will tell if it turns out to be nothing more than a modern name for an indus-trial estate or even the 1930s trading estates.

Like Chatham, the best part of Gillingham is the waterfront; here it is called The Strand, with a fine open view over the estuary and a skyline of the old Hoo Fort on its saltmarsh and the tall tower of Kingsnorth. The A2 goes on into Rainham, where again the area of interest is near the Medway, and we shall meet Lower Rainham in Chapter XIV.

Railways are often regarded as specialist history, but the Box and Cox railway story of the Medway Towns is a most curious part of Kent's history. The riverside area of North Kent had long tempted early railway engineers, like Telford who in 1824 planned a line via Woolwich to Chatham and Dover; in 1832 another plan proposed reaching Chatham by a ferry from Gravesend, and yet another scheme by Vignoles in 1840 suggested reaching the Medway Towns by shallow tunnels underneath Woolwich Arsenal.

At length the South Eastern's North Kent line reached Strood in 1847 by the curious method of a canal tunnel, the story of which belongs in the next chapter. But by January 1850 the S.E.R. was being challenged—and *The Times* reported a large meeting at Rochester—by leading citizens to support a Bill for a line from Strood to Dover. Meanwhile the S.E.R. extended the Maidstone branch to Strood in 1856, but the river was still crossed by ferry. However, a rather shaky concern—the East Kent Railway—had in 1858 joined Faversham to Chatham, and not long afterwards it bridged the river and joined the S.E.R. at Strood. One group of Medway people was pleased with all this, and they were the Army at Chatham, especially the Royal Engineers as they were now much closer to Woolwich.

Dickens now inevitably appears. In "The Uncommercial Traveller", 1861, he refers to his childhood at "Dullborough" (Chatham): "The coach that carried me away, was melodiously called Timpson's Blue-eyed Maid, and . . . the locomotive engine that had brought me back was called severely No 97, and belonged to the S.E.R. (a 2-4-0 built by Cudworth at Ashford in 1846-7) and was spitting ashes and hot water . . ." But here Dickens is hiding his great interest in railways, and anyway as regards names the S.E.R. did have some and the Chatham Railway (ex-East Kent) had nothing but named locomotives. For the East Kent suddenly became the London, Chatham & Dover and by 1860 it had reached London (Victoria) by a series of end-on bits of other people's lines, and the fierce competition with the S.E.R. had begun. This caused traffic on the loop from Rochester to Strood virtually to cease, but a certain Mr Toomer, Mayor of Rochester, agitated successfully in 1876 for it to be resumed, and the curve and its descendants have always been known as the "Toomer Loop".

In 1891, which at the time seemed absurd, the S.E.R. brought the line across an incredible new bridge and into Rochester and Chatham. Neither station was convenient or even necessary, and Chatham Central was in fact a terminal on the outskirts of Rochester! (One railway historian, R. W. Kidner, wrote: ". . . by the less savoury barge-yards".)

Later, under the combined companies (S.E. & C.R.) the two bridges had quite a history, but by 1911 the Old Chatham Bridge and the Toomer Loop were closed, though in 1919 the S.E.R. bridge caught fire, and a great effort had to be made to use the old bridge. Both bridges were used for a time and in 1927 the curves, including "Toomer's" were re-aligned and the S.E.R. bridge used permanently.

Electrification came in 1939—the Mayor of Rochester, Mr Swift, welcoming the decorated motor coach—and afterwards in 1961 extended to the Kent coast. But the old Chatham bridge proved its worth for in 1970 it was used to make a parallel road bridge, as we saw earlier in this chapter.

Interest in air transport started early, for in 1913 Short Brothers, who had come from Leysdown in Sheppey, began building seaplanes—which continued through a long line of famous flying boats. Their works were along the Esplanade and the stretch of water in front saw many famous types taking off and landing, from old biplanes like the "Singapore" to the "Canopus" Empire type. Shorts pioneered the experimental Maia-Mercury composite, which was a small seaplane launched in the air from the larger flying boat, and the "Sunderland" whose fame spread far and wide in the war—a more reliable flying machine was probably never built. Its civilian successor seemed eminently suited to over-water links like the Tasman Sea as well as the River Plate between Buenos Aires and Montevideo, which I knew well. Their decline, like that of the steam locomotive, was forced rather than natural and may well have begun when Shorts were ordered to leave Rochester for Belfast in 1949.

However, Rochester has its own airport high up on the chalk crest which supports modern "Avionics" (electronic aircraft equipment) and there are links with Heathrow and Gatwick; but somehow how much more exciting it would be to arrive at the Medway Towns by air landing on the waters of the river!

My final thoughts on communications are the invisible links provided by the local radio station which has done a great deal in recent years to bind this rather disjointed urban mass of people into a more homogeneous whole, with its historic cathedral, castle and vital dockyard. Local radio certainly proved its worth in times of crisis, and in the tough winter of 1978-9 Radio Medway opened up the station in the small hours to provide an emergency communications centre for Kent because blizzards and then floods had made the area inaccessible. Radio Medway is not just concerned with the Medway Towns themselves, for it covers much of the area of this book right upstream to Tonbridge, and provides the local intimate contact that television lacks.

13

The Hoo Peninsula

This region lies in the angle between the Thames and the Lower Medway and, isolated over the centuries, has a distinctive history. The name Hoo means "spur", and is similar to the much smaller "Hoe" in the West Country estuary of Plymouth Sound, both of them pushing out into water.

If I had written this a few years ago it might have still echoed Richard Church, when he described Hoo in 1948 as "cut off from the mainstream of life even today", and advised those needing "space and silence and solitude" to go there. This advice in part may still hold, but the march of double-quick time has brought the peninsula into the Borough of Medway, and two significant statements in their Guide will explain the change: "Cliffe Woods is being developed as a residential area" and "Hoo St Werburgh now has a large population".

Industry is not new in Hoo, but large settlements are. Small industrial outposts were there long ago, but they didn't greatly alter the character of the landscape. However, change—not always for the best—must follow when very large sprawling housing is attached to small villages, for in spite of their size these estates are isolated and inevitably bring car traffic roaring heedlessly and mindlessly along the narrowish roads of the open marsh landscape, and with it all peace departs.

Not that the landscape is all marsh, for a spinal ridge of low clay hills, sometimes wooded, runs east of Higham to High Halstow and then falls away to Thameside at All Hallows. This ridge rises between two chalk outcrops, northwards at Cliffe and southwards at Frindsbury. Here is a nice little geological point of interest, for the downfolding of the chalk has preserved the clay into hills instead of wearing it away into a valley. Clay makes most of the former Isle of Grain right on the eastern tip of the peninsula which used to be separated by the Yantlet Creek. Here indeed was isolation within isolation, for its earliest history was bound up with water on all sides, inside and outside.

A hint of a remoter tropical past was the discovery of an elephant fossil (*Elephas antiquus*) in the London Clay at Upnor on the Medway; the beasts died here as they do in modern Africa—in the rivers.

The more recent geological history of Hoo has been concerned with the slow rise in sea level after the Roman era and the continual dangers of flooding, which by the thirteenth century meant enclosure of the marshes by walling in order to preserve the marsh pastures. In Saxon times these had formed a whole local economy built up on sheep's wool, meat and ewe's milk for cheese and lasted well into the Middle Ages. The reclaimed sheep pastures have thus been part of the man-made landscape of Hoo for 1200 or 1300 years, and with the saltings, tidal mud flats and creeks make much of the scenery of the river fringes, especially where the remoter open north faces the Thames. Green pastures are often coupled with rainy weather, but here in Hoo it is one of the driest parts of Britain, with rainfall in a year often not reaching even 20 inches (500 millimetres).

The Medway shore is much built on and industrialized, but doesn't lack interest, although the works of man both static and mobile often pollute the salty air with noise. But to understand this mosaic of mud, marsh, man and machinery you must walk and at times wade across the peninsula.

Hoo begins at Frindsbury and from the flint, Roman tile and brick-walled All Saints' Church high on its quarried chalk cliff there is a very good view of the maritime Medway and all its works. Down a lane not far away is a building that reflects a past land use, for it consists of two familiar oast kilns, and in front of them is a beautifully preserved drying loft of slate and brick, with wooden shuttered semi-circular windows, dating from about 1830. Hops have long since disappeared from the region, to be replaced by collards (cabbages) and potatoes in rotation.

Soon you are in Upper Upnor, where the forlorn litter of the foreshore in the shape of decaying concrete barges (from the last war) contrasts with the neatness of the Royal Engineers' establishment, shore and marine. Into the tight and cosy little High Street and suddenly you are confronted with a well-preserved red brick and ragstone castle looming over the muddy riverfront at low tide. This was the 1561 fort of Upnor Castle built to defend the Medway and Chatham Dockyard, but which failed utterly in 1667 to prevent the Dutch invaders from coming up river and burning three English ships. Its greatest excitement had been twenty years earlier when it was captured by the Kentish Royalists. Its useful life ended as a naval ammunition store connected with the long-defunct Chattenden Naval Tramway that ran down to a pier at Lower Upnor.

This shore along to the long strip of Cookham Woods is rather beset with pleasure craft (which I feel are too many, both ashore and afloat) and euphemistically described as a "busy sailing centre". If the Lower Medway must be overwhelmingly dedicated to pleasure craft then I suggest the planners visit Port Grimaud, on a less attractive part of the Côte d'Azur. Here the French have built a Provençal village by the sea in typical vernacular style, but it is also in effect a marina (cleverly disguised); the houses when built were offered at reasonable prices or rentals, and houses and boats blend perfectly.

Beyond Cookham Woods on Hoo mud-flats is a group of "retired" sailing barges. The anchorage and moorings with the shore buildings are rather unsightly, but across the saltings silhouetted against the light the old craft make a nostalgic scene.

Just north of here lies Hoo St Werbergh, one of a group of villages known by the name of their parish church, the main reason now for visiting this overblown settlement. I first saw the church from the river, as it is marked on the Admiralty chart as "conspicuous", which with its fine tower has been so to mariners for centuries. Close to the tower, the hexagonal stair-turret reveals some of its Saxon origin.

Back to the shore and Kingsnorth power station which is an immense but impressive building dominating the estuarine skyline; it was built for economic reasons close to cooling water and waterborne oil fuel, but it is not unlikely that a modern collier may soon be unloading different fuel. Over sixty years ago other large buildings would have been seen; these were the airship sheds of the Navy in the First World War at Kingsnorth, and it must have been quite a sight to watch these huge dirigibles floating away over the estuary to the North Sea to observe for the fleet. North of the power station is the original refinery of Berry Wiggins, who now process bitumen brought from their huge neighbour at Grain.

The landscape is now mud-flats and saltings right up to the Isle of Grain, where Colemouth Creek on the Medway doesn't quite meet the Yantlet coming from the Thames. This estuarine landscape in the summer months at low tide can be quite colourful with saltmarsh plants like ricegrass, the yellow flowers of marsh samphire and the delicate lilacs and pinks of sea lavender and thrift.

In the area near the railway line lies a nice old farmhouse called White Hall, and along the bridle path one autumn evening I met the owner and his dog. He had been retired for many years from North London, loving the solitude of Hoo, and it was from him that I learned of the frightful mess at Grain Power Station which had so distressed the locals for years. Then unknown to the outside world there had been many demarcation disputes and inter-union strikes often accompanied by threats of violence and "go-slows" lasting for months plus unrealistic wage demands.

The island has had a long human history. The first known settlers left behind their Iron Age pottery at Wallend, and the later Teutonic invaders grazed their sheep, and evaporated salt in crude earthen shallow pans filled by the rising tide. Christianity came early too with a wooden church (St James) in the seventh century at Grain, and by Norman times the Yantlet channel was in full use with ragstone cargoes passing to London for the building of the Tower. The marshlands had been embanked against the encroaching estuarine waters, and they formed the ancestors of the present "sea" walls. However, even isolated as they were, the long acquisitive arm of Henry VIII managed to obtain the Manor of Grain at the Dissolution, being an ancient church possession of Canterbury.

The first signs that this lone promontory might have a strategic role came when James II had two batteries put there in case the Prince of Orange might decide on invasion—no doubt with memories of the Dutch raids in his brother's time. However, the first troubles here came not from abroad, but from the City of London when in 1823 the Lord Mayor decided to uphold his ancient rights over the Medway and had the causeway linking Grain with Hoo cut, and the Yantlet channel once more opened. There was a terrific protest from farmers and landowners and they got the Crown to contest their case at the Surrey Assizes a year later, and the jury found the Corporation guilty and Grain once more was no longer an island. The curious thing is that a tradition or legend exists of a high-arched bridge over the channel, but there is no record of it. The defence problem remained, however, and in 1866 a fort and a garrison were established.

In 1882 the South Eastern Railway reached Grain from Gravesend, and Port Victoria, a 400-foot (125-metre) wooden pier sticking out into the river Medway, was created. This was not so much for the defence of Chatham (as had been suggested by a Colonel Jervis at the War Office in 1865) but as part of the "cold war" against their rivals the Chatham & Dover Company. This was to try and take advantage of the Dutch steamers from

Queenborough to Flushing which ran in connection with the Chatham Company; the S.E.R.'s passengers were ferried across the Medway to the steamers.

This service was a failure, but not so the branch, and Port Victoria became a Royal favourite, particularly with Queen Victoria. She loved it for she could embark on the Royal Yacht, and as she said, "not be met by vast screaming crowds"; the S.E.R. even kept a crimson carpet in the little wooden station there. The Royal Corinthian Yacht Club went there too, and even built a club house, and a number of royal special trains used to run direct from Windsor without stopping—a rail link managed with great ingenuity—and then down the grimy North Kent line to this South Eastern outpost of great hopes. But being an outpost the pier was often damaged—badly by a gale in 1897 when the island was completely flooded. Eventually the station was moved back to dry land in 1916, the pier and port closed, but trains ran there until 1951. Ironically the last royal person to use Port Victoria was the Kaiser in 1911 on his way home after George V's Coronation; he must have liked it too for along with Edward VII and Queen Alexandra he contributed to the restoration of the ancient church of St James at Grain.

The presence of oil on the island is not new, for in 1912 Churchill with his usual foresight persuaded the Admiralty to have oil-storage tanks put there (still in use), and so began the birth of an oil-fired Navy; later in 1914 the Royal Naval Air Service came, as at Kingsnorth.

The first refinery in 1923 was a small enterprise run by an American, Charles Ganahl, who bought marshland at Wallend and tried out a pioneer system of "cracking" petroleum liquids— in this case Russian paraffin—which lasted until 1932 when it shut down. But the valuable installations like the barge jetty and storage continued to be used and expanded underground, so that by 1944 they were part of the famous "Pluto" pipeline pumping petrol under the Channel to the Allied armies in France. This and the defunct Port Victoria were swallowed up in 1953 by the huge B.P. Refinery which had the site raised by Dutch engineers—well used to these sorts of areas—who pumped sand ashore to make it.

Over the years I have often seen the refinery, especially at night when the cracking tower lights made it appear as a city of the future. When at last I got inside to see it the impression was of clinical robot cleanliness and efficiency—for man was no- where to be seen! I was keen to see a supertanker close up, for nearly a quarter of a century earlier I had served in a mere 17,000-tonner in the Caribbean. Mr Thomas, the Information Officer, kindly took me down to the Marine Terminal with its many jetties to see the 260,000-ton *British Trident* that was unloading her part cargo of 100,000 tons of crude oil from Kuwait. The river, though deep, is not deep enough for these monsters when fully loaded; they are so long that they have to be berthed by hydraulic rams. Coming back I saw a stretch of reed-fringed water with many wildfowl, including breeding swans. Mr Thomas explained, "They're happy enough, a refinery is a quiet place, you know", and indeed it is; more noise is made by the staff arriving and departing in their cars.

The refinery uses an enormous amount of water, 2 million gallons a day for the actual refining and 5 million gallons an hour for cooling, drawn from the salty, dirty Medway. This is discharged back after cleaning by separators, often much cleaner than when first drawn.

Next door in contrast to this quiet activity is the gaunt white elephant of Grain Power Station—a silent monument to the ineffectual mammoth organizations whose conscience for public money seems as tiny as the conscience of trade unions to disrupt; add in the myth of cheap oil and inflation and the whole thing has led to the demise of a monster of modern technology.

Beyond here is the tip of the Medway left bank now meeting the Thames after its 70-mile (112-kilometre) journey from the High Weald of Sussex. Westwards from Grain and across the Yantlet is the expanded village of Lower Stoke, and northwards again is All Hallows, whose ancient church was one of six here at Domesday. Over the marsh pastures and on the banks of the Thames are the serried ranks of chalets and caravans which have inherited the former Southern Railway's attempt to create a resort here by extending a short branch from Middle Stoke to near a waterside farm. It might have succeeded, but the war and the motor-car killed it off, and the slow but pleasant journey through the orchards and little halts with names like Sharnal Street and Beluncle has gone for ever. The cynics said it was Thames mud versus Thanet sand, but the real winners were the car and the caravans.

From All Hallows there is a back road where, dodging the intermittent zooming traffic, I came across the beautiful restored 1680 William and Mary Brickhouse Farm that for many years belonged to the Everest family. In the front garden the present owner's wife, Mrs Marsh, told me that such was the isolation even in the late nineteenth century that there were but three literate people in the parish, and smuggling still flourished. The open fields and dry climate are ideal for corn and vegetables, and before the war the artist Rowland Hilder lived here in a caravan whilst painting in the area. Dagenham Farm nearby has a house of the same period which shows that the Hoo farmers were as much yeomen as their fellows further south in the Weald. Westwards and higher is St Mary's Hoo, splendidly unspoiled but its deconsecrated church looks forlorn. Inside is a fine 1914-18 war memorial in the reredos among the disused clutter.

On the rising land is High Halstow with a good pub, and from Northward Hill Nature Reserve are some sweeping views of the varied Hoo landscape. Soon we are in Cooling and the country of *Great Expectations*, with its churchyard and the thirteen small stone lozenge tombs of a family completely wiped out in the 1770s—from what indeed, one wonders? There were of course several endemic complaints in Hoo; marsh "ague" was one and mosquitoes further east from the First World War were only recently eradicated by the local health people. Dickens, however, took only five graves for Pip's family: perhaps he didn't wish to copy nature too much. The church is deconsecrated and firmly locked, the churchyard now rather unkempt but there is still that air of mystery which must have been even stronger in Dickens's day.

Cooling has a famous fourteenth-century castle ruin which was an earlier manor house crenellated by Sir John de Cobham to defend the estuary—a bit late in the day after the previous French raids. The battlements and machiolations on the twin circular gatehouses are some of the best-preserved examples of this sort of fortifying in all Kent. The builder's plaque in the east tower seems to have worried some people; it is late Middle English, which of course still contains old French and merely states what the castle was built for. The builder wasn't to know that its career would be like Upnor's, not of great use nationally but mixed up with religious rebels like the Lollard Sir John Oldcastle in 1414 who owned it, and our Reformationist Sir Thomas Wyatt who attacked it in 1554. Inside is interesting as water still laps the curtain wall, and beyond is a garden with a cabbage palm tree.

After Cooling, Cliffe, from the Saxon Clyva—rather obviously as it is at the top of a chalk cliff—with a High Street full of Kentish weatherboarding. There are rather too many new houses, but Cliffe is interesting because of its large church and its Roman origin. The Roman beginnings are seen in the pattern of the fields, called centuriation (rectangular blocks), which they used for growing corn on the light chalky fertile soils for the town and their garrison at Rochester. The pattern was kept and merged into the Saxon strip farming, and its consequent open field remained down the centuries until in 1778 it was the largest field in Kent (2,000 acres; 800 hectares). It was still there in 1840, and the bordering straight roads are witness to its origin.

The church walls show a pattern resulting from two Kentish limey rocks—flints and ragstone. Inside is light and airy with superb stonework and the baptistry has stone seating for the older and infirm parishioners, which in churches gives rise to the saying "Weakest to the wall". The splendid clean condition of everything and the flowers are due to ladies that go in and out all day to watch over the church's safety. Alas for this vigilance! I read in the paper not long afterwards that there had been a bad case of vandalism, which so upset the vicar that he felt a much greater effort ought to be made to find the culprits, instead of lamenting the act passively.

From Cliffe to Higham (really Lower Higham), where the station was much used by Dickens. It is at the north end of the unusual canal tunnel more than two miles long that was such a great asset to the old Thames and Medway Canal of 1824 that ran from Frindsbury Basin to near Gravesend. In 1845, seeing the inevitable end, the company turned itself into a railway and put a line along the towpath balanced on piles driven into the water. Not long after they were absorbed into the S.E.R., as we saw earlier. The track was doubled by draining and filling in the bed—quite an effort to fill a hole two miles long by eight feet deep! There are now two tunnels, and a fifty-yard gap in a deep cutting which was where the old barge passing place used to be. I found this rather exciting relic of a vanished waterway by cycling over the fields and paths, and with a bit of mountaineering was able to see it.

Before we pass on to Gads Hill beyond Higham, and plunge into the nostalgia of Dickens, it is interesting to recall the legend of Dick Turpin that originated here. In 1676 a man named Nicks on a bay horse robbed a gentleman at 4 a.m. on Gads Hill, crossed the Thames by the Gravesend ferry and after a tumultuous ride cross-country via Essex and Huntingdon, with brief stops for sleep and his horse, arrived at York that same afternoon. There he changed his clothes and deliberately met the Lord Mayor on the bowling green, making himself conspicuous by remarks and asking the time rather pointedly. The inevitable prosecution came later, the York mayor testified and Nicks was acquitted, on the grounds of the impossibility of being in two places so remote on the same day. Charles II was keenly interested and on being promised pardon Nicks revealed the truth, whereupon his majesty dubbed him "Swift Nicks".

Gads Hill is Dickens, and Gadshill Place (now a girls' school) was the house Dickens so longed for. He had previously brought it into fiction in *A Christmas Carol*; it became his at last and in 1858 he wrote to his French friend, Monsieur Cerjat, to say he was "on my little Kentish free-hold . . ." In the grounds used to be the Swiss chalet, given to him by the actor Fechter, where he wrote in the summer; for a while it was at Cobham Park given by the Dickens family after his death to Lord Darnley. There was also a balustrade from the old Rochester bridge given to Dickens when it was blown up. I suppose it was inevitable that new houses nearby would be in roads such as Copperfield Crescent, Charles Dickens Drive and Little Dorritt!

Overall of course still hangs the spirit of Shakespeare's Falstaff, commemorated in the pub opposite, but it is a sobering reflection that the last thirty years have almost obliterated the previous three hundred.

At length we come to Strood, a town Dickens mentioned briefly in *The Pickwick Papers*, and as Scrooge's home (disguised) in *A Christmas Carol*.

14

Across the Swale to Sheppey

The most interesting way out of the Medway Towns to the east, other than by water, is by Lower Rainham, a very different place from the busy upper part strung out along the A2, Watling Street. There are some old buildings here like the 1420 Bloors Place which is an intriguing mixture of hung tiles, Georgian alterations and Victorian additions. The outer walls were loop-holed against seaborne raiders or smugglers in Tudor times—not the most friendly people. A much more recent building but of unusual design is Wakeley's Oasts, a large long four-storey block with a slate roof and used for storing hops and grain; it is now the Rainham Community Centre. Here south of the main railway line is a world of Medway creeks, mud with marsh seawards and orchards inshore. Seeing one of the railway bridges reminded me of a strange wartime accident in 1944 when a Spitfire pilot, desperately trying to deviate a "Doodle-bug" (V1 rocket) from its course, only succeeded by tipping it with his wings down on to an express train crossing a bridge. There were eight killed, and a young woman I knew who was a passenger was laid out amongst the victims, although she was unhurt and only stunned.

Not far along is Otterham Quay with a little coaster terminal at the head of the creek, and on the other side are orchards which used to be full of cherry trees. This fruit, as we have seen, seems to present modern growers with many difficulties, so large numbers have turned over to growing Conference pears. Many of these are on the peninsula that juts out into the estuary, the centre of which is the village of Upchurch on a small hill. This village, like so many now, has an interesting church, some pleasant houses and a lot of plain ones. St Mary's Church with its "candle-snuffer" steeple—a well-worn phrase though it seems the best description—dominates the centre. The most notable vicar here was Edmund Drake, in 1560 from Tavistock in Devon, a naval chaplain who had twelve sons; the eldest, Sir Francis (as he became), was one of the greatest seafarers or pirates—depending on your point of view—in English history.

Across the fields one can reach Lower Halstow, but I walked to Ham Green among the orchards and then along the saltings of

Twinney Creek. This area from Lower Rainham through Up-church to Lower Halstow has sometimes been called the Lost Lands for in Roman times what are now alluvial flats were much higher, and have become "drowned" as the sea level has risen (or the earth's crust depressed) since then. It was an extensive pottery and brickfield during the third and fourth centuries, and Red Samian ware among much coarse pottery has been found.

Along the way are moored some interesting old craft, either lived in or for occasional use. I met a very cheerful Danish lady in one married to a Geordie who gave me coffee—she has been here nearly twenty years. And right among the orchards which are near the water's edge I came across the refurbished barge *Mayflower* resting elegantly on the flats.

From here across Barksore and Chetney Marshes the flats are very extensive and at low tide you can see how a plant succession builds up. The pioneer species is usually the marsh sam-phire with yellow flowers, and is soon followed by ricegrass (*Spartina townsendii*) whose roots go down deeply into the soft mud; it has spread at a very rapid rate around the estuaries and creeks of the south and east coasts since it was first seen about a century ago in Southampton Water. No other salt-marsh plant has so rapid and so great an influence in gaining land from the sea.

Lower Halstow's name is from Halgastow meaning Halig Stow or holy place, but it may not necessarily have been origin-ally a Christian one, for this is an old area of Roman settlement, and just inland from here were villas at Hartlip, Boxley and Borden. The church of St Margaret of Antioch, an unusual dedication—although there are two others locally—gives a hint of how old Christianity is in these parts. There is a strong possibility that some of the building might even be Roman (Christian), as on the south wall of the chancel is a small blocked window of Roman tiles. The outside is not particularly Kentish in appearance, but from seawards it fits in well with the wind-swept marshy landscape: low walls, squat pointed tower, small windows and doors. Its most valued possession is the lead font from about 1160, and only rediscovered by accident in 1921 when its plaster covering cracked open. Why it had been covered up is a mystery; lead fonts are rare—in the whole of Britain there are only about thirty—and this might be the oldest. Poss-ibly it was hidden from prying Cromwellian eyes as church articles were often melted down during the Commonwealth.

Modern Lower Halstow's chief interests are this old church besides its muddy creek and 1633 Church Cottage with two much later houses, now smartly painted, Mandarin Lodge and Britannia House, plus a strip of tarmac called the "tramway" and the Roman history of pottery and obscure early Christianity. The former Eastwoods Brickworks tramway carried bricks to be loaded into Medway barges, and represented an old industry (apart from Roman workings) from the mid-seventeenth century onwards when the dockyard demands were high; it closed in 1966. This seems to have sparked off the usual dreary private estates swelling the population of what had been a decaying parish up to 1,100 by 1977. The latest piece of speculation is to have a marina with 20 detached houses, parking for 800 cars and moorings for 700 boats, which will give the estuary little peace, but perhaps the Parish Council will object.

From Lower Halstow there is a pleasant climb up to Callum Hill with a good view out over the estuary of orchards, pasture, marsh and saltings. Before going on to Sheppey, a walk through the orchards will bring you to the small village of Bobbing. This place may be one of the earliest Saxon settlements in Kent or for that matter England, because in 450 a group of farmers landed at Milton Creek. They made their way through Romano-British cultivated land to settle here, the village name meaning "Bobba's people".

Here we are on the main Sheerness road (A249) which is dreadfully noisy, but other than by train there is no other route, except a side road via Funton and more brickworks which is often closed. Soon the high steel and concrete structure of Kingsferry road and rail lift bridge appears, a Swale crossing that has had quite a history during the last 120 years. In 1860 the Chatham & Dover Railway came to Sheppey, the dockyard at Sheerness being the original object, and as the company built the first bridge they acquired the ancient rights of "Wardens and Jury of the King's Ferry".

The old bridge had a swing section, and was destined to have an adventurous life, for with the development of railways, ships also got bigger and more traffic used the Swale channel. In 1904 it was therefore reconstructed; then in 1922 there was a serious collision, and railway and road were out of action for ten months. This was the prelude to a lot more, usually in fog by paper and pulp vessels from Ridham Dock, especially after the last war, and the 1953 tidal surge and consequent floods didn't help. By 1960 reconstruction was more than necessary—a new bridge was urgently needed—so this time a smart lift type was built which can give a clearance of 90 feet (10½ metres) when the centre section is raised.

This first sight of Sheppey—the Isle of Sheep (from Scaep)—at its western end is not inspiring, but a closer look, and ignoring the heavy traffic on the main road, shows that there are things to see in this Medway outpost. Geologically the island is a great lump of London Clay across its northern half rising to its highest point at 240 feet (73 metres) near Minster along a ridge, with a line of eroded cliffs along its north coast, and falling away to a great expanse of flat open marsh and pasture in its southern half. The crumbling clay cliffs are full of fossils, especially tropical plants and warm-water creatures like turtles and sharks.

Sheppey's early history is bound up with raids and religion, for in 674 the Queen of Kent, Sexburgha, had established an abbey church and nunnery at what is now Minster. In 835 the Danes raided the island and burnt it, and twenty years later felt bold or safe enough to stay there throughout the winter. In 1052 Earl Godwin and his son Harold, the future king, repeated the Danish destruction and destroyed it again when they were in revolt against the English king, who happened to be Edward the Confessor. The soft clay cliffs have steadily been eaten away by the sea, for in 1780 Minster was in the centre of the island, which was at that time surrounded by walls.

After the bridge comes Queenborough which in recent years has welcomed its visitors, particularly those arriving by train, with the all-pervading aroma of the glue works. This little ex-borough has become even more heavily industrialized recently with a rolling mill built at Rushenden in 1972, adding to the older industry of glass-making (now the largest factory in the South-East) and earlier there was an iron pyrites factory, as far back as the 1600s in fact, from the copperas stones found in the London Clay; this lasted until the nineteenth century. However, there is quite a lot of history here, and things worth seeing.

Queenborough's history begins with coastal defence, for Edward III built a castle, and a good one from all accounts, in 1366 near the present station, and a royal borough was created. But Queenborough, like Lenham, became a failed town, and two hundred years later there were but a score of houses. But the place had its share of excitement for in 1580 an Armada treasure ship was brought here and its commander, Don Cerinimo, was made a prisoner of war and never saw Spain again for he died in 1591. In 1620 a totally different sort of vessel arrived, this time made of brown paper and kept afloat by two stockfish and eight bladders. It had been paddled down from London by two watermen, one of whom was a poet called Taylor.

The castle seems to have annoyed Cromwell, as other castles did, and he had it utterly destroyed in 1648. Not long afterwards came the greatest excitement of all with the raid by the Dutch Navy under the resolute and fearless De Ruyter who appeared off the Nore on 10th June 1667 and attacked Sheerness fort which resisted, but when a large Dutch force of 800 men landed the garrison fled and the fort was captured. On or about the 11th Queenborough seems to have surrendered for which much opprobrium has been cast upon it, but one must remember that there was a thriving oyster trade with Holland—plus much smuggling which continued for another 150 years. This was also a rather foolish war which England had got herself into with her erstwhile ally, partly over the chauvinistic Navigation Acts; and as she was also thoroughly unprepared, no doubt the inhabitants of Queenborough felt that discretion was the better part of valour. On the 12th the Dutch sailed up the Medway, captured the *Unity* and broke the famous chain at Chatham, which didn't seem very effective (for many years a bolt allegedly from it was displayed in Holland) and after exchange of fire captured the 82-gun ship *Royal Charles*. On the 13th they re-rigged the *Royal Charles* and with the *Unity* sailed for Holland, but they were in control of part of Kent for some weeks after. All this caused a great outburst of anger and dismay, with threats like "Commissioner Petts ought to be hanged!" (the incident of the four horses drawing a piece of wood at Chatham, described in Chapter XII). After other raids peace was at length signed at Breda, but the whole affair had thoroughly alarmed the nation and the Medway Towns in particular.

Queenborough continued to annoy people. Defoe was very rude about the place in 1724, calling it a "miserable, dirty, decay'd poor, pitiful, fishing town". What really upset him, being a Londoner, was the fact that they had two Members of Parliament, "as many as the Borough of Southwark, or the City of Westminster". In 1729 Queenborough supplied the Navy with water from the well of the destroyed castle.

In 1876 the town came to life again with the Chatham Company who transferred their new Continental service from Sheerness to a long pier in the Swale. The ships were run by the Dutch Zeeland Company to Vlissingen (Flushing); the company was a great triumph for Chairman Forbes (he had been Manager of the Dutch Rhenish Railway at one time), and one in the eye for the S.E.R. The pier, however, had a career rather like the town, for it was burnt down in 1882, suffered flooding in 1897, and got burnt again in 1900. The night service was transferred to Folkestone in 1911 (during all these upsets it had gone temporarily to Dover and later to Port Victoria). The First World War killed the service and it left Queenborough for good afterwards, and in 1926 the Zeeland Company had had enough of Kent and transferred their base to Harwich.

By now the town had long lost its Members of Parliament and shared an M.P. with Faversham, and the final indignity came with the 1974 Act which ended its municipal status and made it part of the Swale District Council centred, to its and Sheerness's chagrin, at Sittingbourne. So now the fine little eighteenth-century Guildhall is just another building, but the town in spite of noise, industry and that modern horror—an industrial estate —has a nice little High Street. In it are some good Georgian houses, the 1702 Church House where Lady Hamilton stayed when she visited Nelson, and another of 1706; but the house that attracted me was a neat one of 1850 called Fig Tree House, nicely painted in green and white with an actual fig tree in the front garden.

From Queenborough at one time a light railway ran across the island to the straggling "resort" of Leysdown with seven halts; it lasted just fifty years, being closed by the Southern Region in 1950, its failure mainly being due to lack of goods traffic. But, thirty years later, a line like this if operated by steam would surely pay—if only in the summer months.

It is not far along the river front to Sheerness overlooking the Lappel Bank which is being reclaimed for deep-water terminal sites by the new commercial port. Sheerness means "bright headland", which some would dispute as its first appearance is grim and dirty, but there is more history here than in many a fairer spot. Before we embark on the dockyard story, to the right are the 1972 steelworks, making steel from scrap, a big employer; its capacity is 3 per cent of the United Kingdom's, and like all steelworks it is under a shadow.

After the demise of the unfortunate battery in 1667, more attention was paid to the dockyard that had been begun in 1665 with new repair docks surveyed by Pepys himself. But the area was isolated and smuggling rampant, for in 1783 the House of Commons learned: "There is not one excise officer at Sheerness, where, and in the River Medway, the revenue loses £50,000 per annum. Which trade has so increased, as nearly all the spirits, wine, tea, tobacco, raisins etc consumed in that neighbourhood are smuggled . . ." Then with the Napoleonic Wars came great activity, and a new threat to the country's security arose, not from a foreign enemy but a serious mutiny at the Nore in 1797 due to atrocious conditions in the Fleet, and people saw hoisted, perhaps for the first time, a red flag on some of the off-lying warships.

In 1805 the body of England's greatest admiral returned home to Sheerness in a barrel of spirits of wine (alcohol) from Gibraltar, having been brought from his flagship, H.M.S. *Victory* (built at Chatham in 1765), in a cask of brandy to Gibraltar. His coffin was made here from the mainmast of the *L'Orient* and taken in a yacht to Chatham and thence to Greenwich.

It was during these wars from 1813 onwards that the dock-yard was developed into a naval base. The construction was of a high quality and carried out under Rennie. The whole of the foundations, with a river wall of dressed granite facing the river Medway, was on piling with coffer-dams carried out in the deepest water ever attempted. Two ingenious machines were designed by Rennie for use in the piling, one for tongueing and grooving and the other as a pile cutter. The materials specified were of a high quality such as "well burnt Dorking or Halling lime" and "well dressed granite masonry from Cornwall, Devon-shire or Aberdeen".

From this time onwards the river Medway became full of the famous hulks (some were known as Shear or Sheer hulks being fitted with shears for hoisting, hence the sea shanty: "Here, a sheer hulk, lies poor Tom Bowling . . .") which were a familiar sight to Dickens off Upnor. The main anchorage was in Stan-gate Creek where they were used for hospitals, houseboats, quarantine, prisoners of war and later of course for convicts. Sometimes they stretched from Sheerness to Rochester, and many were still seaworthy but laid up.

Then the dockyard saw two world wars and finally in 1961, after nearly three hundred years, the Navy relinquished it on the grounds of economy. My wife, who lived in the dockyard when she was a schoolgirl, had many memories of it, but she says two stand out: the early morning mass of bicycles arriving and ten minutes later the stillness while the dockyard mateys had their breakfast, and the other is that the place was rarely free from a wind blowing—for the island is very exposed. My memories are short and not very sweet, as in 1946 I was sent along with the First Lieutenant of our submarine to see a naval surgeon and have our ears cleaned out following painful ear-ache whilst the boat lay on the bed of the river Medway.

The great surge and floods of 1953 were disastrous in Sheppey when the waters of the Thames and Medway estuaries poured through the sea defences at 3 a.m. on 31st January and cut off the island. In the Sheppey rural district twenty-one families had to be rescued by boat including the old lady licensee from the upper-floor window of the ancient pub, the "Lord Nelson" (now gone), near Kingsferry Bridge. However, there was a lighter side to these events for the Naval Chaplain at the dock-yard, an Irishman, lost all his sermons in the rising waters, and was heard to remark: "Arl the beautiful t'oughts of twinty years went floating down the road!"

Today Sheerness is a modern commercial port with dynamic growth, using a mixture of the latest shipping techniques: pal-letizing, containers and LASH (lighter aboard ship) and a RoRo (roll on/roll off) terminal which the largest car-carrier in the world uses—the Japanese *Jinyu Maru*. New deep-water berths front the river which will take vessels of 11.5 metres (about 38 feet) draught at low tide, a valuable asset for a tidal port. There is a new ferry terminal used mainly by the modern inheritors of the old railway service to Vlissingen. This is the Olau Company, started from scratch at the time of Suez by an enterprising Dane, Ole Lauritzen, and built up into an extraordinarily suc-cessful, thoroughly international freight and passenger busi-ness, which originally worked from Ramsgate and came to Sheerness in 1975. The new service was a phenomenal success; distance (108 nautical miles) and time didn't seem to worry the users, but I think one of the reasons was the completion of the vast 25-year Dutch Delta Plan. This was started after the ter-rible floods of 1953, and embraced flood control by new dams with motorways on them and ended, for better or worse, the centuries-old isolation of the water-grit province of Zeeland.

I talked with Mr Case Rietkirk, the Dutch-born General Man-ager at Sheerness of Olau Lines, and he was optimistic about the port's future and his company's services, especially because the vast increase in traffic has caused the company to build a huge 13,500-ton "luxury" ferry with seven decks, the *Olau Hollandia* at Bremerhaven in Germany, with economical engines and modern berthing arrangements (like bow thrusters) and a speed of 22 knots. He admitted to having reservations about restrictive union practices, but he has managed to get good labour relations, although it amounts to paying very high rates for about ten minutes' actual loading time on the night crossings.

On the debit side of the new port I thought there had been some rather ruthless destruction of the well-built Georgian dockyard buildings, but the Docks Manager, Mr Dixon, told me that a modern port needs just a vast spread of concrete and specialized storage sheds—which is doubtless correct, if rather stark. The other thing that perturbed me was that, whilst admiring the Japanese efficiency and enterprise, I shuddered at the thought of all these new cars cluttering up the roads of the Weald and Medway area.

Sheerness town is unattractive, but there is a curious atmosphere about the place that is reminiscent of old-time England and North Kent, when the Services were more prominent than they are today. There is a little fish restaurant in the High Street where I had one of the best fish dishes I've ever eaten; the place was clean, cheap and very cheerful. But my wife said Sheerness was always so, grim town but pleasant people.

From the town there are two diversions, interesting and not far off. Out via Minster to St Sexburgha's Church and then along to the ruins of Shurland Castle. This is old, decayed and impressive being full of legends, but all that exists now is a large brick gatehouse lived in by Henry VIII's Lord Treasurer, Sir Thomas Cheyney. Like Brambletye, it has been a ruin for 300 years. I talked to the farmer who has Shurland Farm (which includes the ruins), some 300 acres (120 hectares) with 400 sheep, and his biggest problem in this rural area is in the summer time with an adjacent caravan site with 1500 caravans on it. There is a pleasant little pond in front of this ruin, but the former elms have all succumbed to the recent disease, so he has planted some new trees to maintain the beauty of the site. He told me that many people come to survey the ruin for potential restoration, but few are interested—the cost would be excessive. On the way back, have a look at the curiously named Scocles Farm, a most delightful brick farmhouse with a porticoed doorway and fine dormer windows; outside the front garden wall is a large mounting block.

Our last venture will be to walk out along the beach to Garrison Point, the furthest bit of the right bank of the river, and look up at the Medway Port Operations Centre and Radar Station, and reflect on the river we have just come down from far-off wooded Sussex.

Whilst I was there the last time I had an unexpected pleasure of seeing a red-sailed Medway barge tacking across the estuary to continue its voyage to East Anglia. Thus the Medway of the past went by the Medway of the present (the Radar Station), but whatever happens to man and his works, the river is timeless.

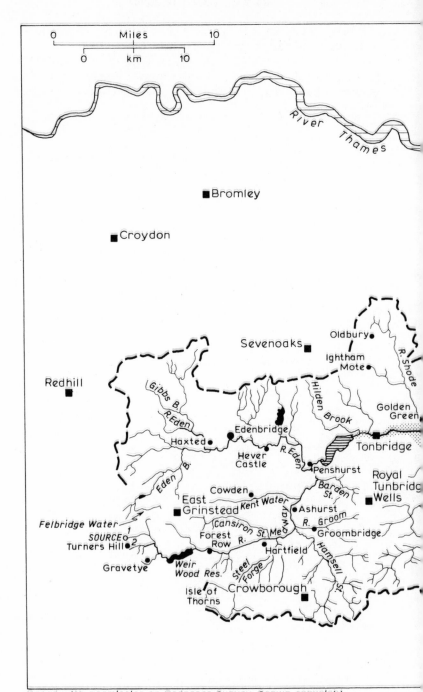

Based with permission on Ordnance Survey. Crown copyright.

Cliffe

HOO
PENINSULA

Hoo
St. Werburgh

Gads
Hill

Upnor
Castle

Cobham

Rochester

Gillingham

Chatham

Wouldham

odland

R. Medway

Eccles

Aylesford

West
Malling

Maidstone

Teston

E. Farleigh

Mereworth

Nettlestead

Yalding

R. Beult

R. Twist

R. Teise

Mote
Park
Lake

R. Len

R. Loose

Leeds Castle

Affers
Wood

Headcorn

R. Sherway

Hammer St.

Smarden

R. Beult

Sissinghurst Castle

Lamberhurst

R. Bewl

R. Tee

Bewl
Bridge Res.

Yantlet Creek

Isle of
Grain

Garrison Pt.

Sheerness

Queensborough

ISLE OF SHEPPEY

Lower
Halstow

The
Swale

Ashford

Great
Chart

Miswell Wood   1

Butcher's Wood   2

Boundary of
catchment area   — — —

Reservoir storage area ≡≡≡

Flood plain protected
by the scheme

Index

Horsted Keynes, 23, 30
Howard, Catherine, 94, 135
Hoys, 15
Huguenots, 85, 92, 159–60
Hunton, 85, 104, 109
Hunton Court, 109
Hussey family, 102
Hythe, 127; beds, 105, 111, 131, 136

Ice Ages, 12, 13, 24, 32, 57, 64, 90, 94, 111, 123, 148
Ightham, 13, 72, 90
Ightham Court, 90
Ightham Mote, 92–3, 107
Iron Age, 14, 25, 45, 46, 56, 64, 69, 72, 81, 91, 111, 131
Ironworking, 15, 26–8, 30–1, 33, 36, 40, 41, 42–3, 44, 45–6, 47, 48, 49, 55, 56–7, 58, 59, 71, 73, 77, 78, 83–4, 98, 99, 100, 102, 103, 104, 107, 126, 145, 153; bloomeries (Celtic), 26, 56, 65, (Roman), 26–7, 30, 42–3, 44, 45–6, (post-Roman), 28, 33, 84; cannon, 15, 28, 37, 47, 55, 71, 78, 83, 100, 103, 145; firebacks, 57, 100; forges & furnaces (Tudor & later), 28, 30, 31, 33, 36, 40, 41, 44, 47, 48, 49, 55, 56–7, 58, 77, 78, 83–4, 99, 100, 102, 103; graveslabs, 31, 35, 57

Jacobean, 35, 36, 83, 84, 117
Jacobites, 62, 106, 115
James I, King, 150, 155
James II, King, 50, 160, 168
Japan & Japanese, 76, 119, 161, 181, 182
Jerrold, Walter, 60, 106
Judde, Sir Andrew, 77
Jutes, 15, 69, 133

Kent College, 88
"Kent, Men of", 55–6, 127, 157
Kent River Board (Southern Water), 21, 67, 156
Kent, Vale of, 66
Kent Water, River, 55, 56–7
"Kentish Men", 55–6
Kentish rag (ragstone), 15, 60, 68, 86, 91, 94, 98, 105, 106, 107, 111, 115, 123, 126, 128, 131, 132, 135, 136, 141, 144, 147, 168, 172
Kettle Corner & Bridge, 122
Kew Gardens, 24
Kid Brook, 38
Kidbrooke Park, 38–9
Kingscote, 30–1
Kingsferry Bridge, 176–7
Kingsnorth, 162, 167, 169
Kit's Coty, 15, 147
Knickpoints, 132, 134

Laddingford, 104
Lamb, Professor H., 85
Lambarde, William, 21, 58, 104–5

Lamberhurst, 100, 101
Langley, 136
Langley church, 131
Latrobe, Benjamin, 17, 40, 42
Leeds Castle, 134–5
Leeds Church (St Nicholas') & Priory, 135
Leigh, 66, 68
Len, River, 13, 125, 127, 131, 132–5, 136, 137
Lenham, 132–3, 177
Lewes, 38, 46, 60, 100
Leyswood, 50–1
Limpsfield, 58
Lingfield, 59
Little Ice Age, the, 85
Little Mill, 96
Locks, 72, 83, 88, 89, 98, 118, 123, 128, 141
London, 16, 22, 23, 30, 36, 61, 65, 74, 75, 76, 77, 79, 81, 83, 85, 88, 115, 126, 127, 128, 130, 137, 142, 154, 155, 156, 157, 159, 162, 168, 178; City of, 157; Lord Mayors of, 61, 65, 77, 156–7, 168; Tower of, 15, 142, 168
Loose stream, 13, 125, 131–2, 136, 137
Loose village, 132
"Lord Nelson" pub (Sheppey), 181
Lorraine, 41
Lower Halstow, 16, 174, 175–6
Lower Halstow church (St Margaret of Antioch), 175, 176
Lower Rainham, 174, 175
Luddesdown Court & village, 151

Magna Carta, 15
Maidstone, 13, 14, 15, 16, 71, 72, 74, 83, 85, 87, 88, 98, 111, 119, 123, 124, 125–31, 132, 137, 141, 145, 148, 153, 156, 162; bridges, 126, 130; Church (All Saints), 126; College, 126; Mote Park, 13, 129, 137; Navigation, 71, 72, 128; Railways, 87, 88, 129–30, 162
Marne, River, 21
Mary Tudor, Queen, 33, 108, 126, 142, 158
Maupassant, Guy de, 89
Maxwell, Donald, 22
Meanders (incised), 57, 63, 135
Mereworth, 114, 115–16; Castle, 116–17, 134; Church (St Lawrence), 115–16; Mere House, 115
Mills (water), 15, 29, 36, 47, 51, 52, 55, 56, 57, 58, 59, 60, 66–7, 71, 96–7, 125, 132, 134, 136; (corn & flour), 43, 51, 55, 59, 132, 160–1; (paper), 57, 91, 92, 128, 132, 137, 145–6; (wind), 43, 160–1
Millhall, 145, 153
Milne, A. A., 47
Milton Creek, 176
Minster (Sheppey), 177, 182
Miswell Wood, 21, 22
Monkton, Viscount, 133
Monterey Pine (California), 92
Motorways, 82, 90, 130, 143, 146, 149